100 THINGS TO DO IN BENTONVILLE/ROGERS BEFORE YOU DIE

Mural in Downtown Rogers

100 THINGS TO DO IN BENTONVILLE/ROGERS BEFORE YOU DIE

CONNIE COTTINGHAM

REEDY PRESS

Reedy Press
PO Box 5131
St. Louis, MO 63139, USA
reedypress.com

Library of Congress Control Number: 2024939001

ISBN: 9781681065335

Design by Jill Halpin

Printed in the United States of America
24 25 26 27 28 5 4 3 2 1

DEDICATION

To my amazing network of friends from which there was a constant outpouring of encouragement as I wrote this book. To the other authors of Reedy Press books, who lift each other up and generously share ideas. And to everyone in this area who smiled and said, "Yes, we need this book." I appreciate you all.

Nola's Pantry in Rogers

CONTENTS

Introduction .... **xv**

Food and Drink

1. Drive through the Very First Location of 7 Brew **2**

2. Take a Shopping Break at Artisan Wood Fired Kitchen **3**

3. Indulge at Baked by Kori **4**

4. Experience Farm-to-Table Fine Dining at Conifer **5**

5. Think about Crystal Bridges as Another Place for Coffee at Eleven **6**

6. Plan a Pizza Night Out at Gusano's Chicago-Style Pizzeria **7**

7. Try a Sandwich at Iron Horse Coffee Company **8**

8. Feel at Home in Jaclyn's Kitchen **9**

9. Watch the Planes While Having Lunch at Louise **10**

10. Indulge in Award-Winning Fried Chicken at Monte Ne Inn **12**

11. Pick Up Lunch, Ideas, and Ingredients at Nola's Pantry **14**

12. Drink Beer, Do Good at Ozark Beer Company **15**

13. Cozy Up with Freshly Baked Goodness at Olly Makes Bakery **16**

14. Go Beyond the Familiar at Bentonville Taco & Tamale Co. **17**

15. Relax with Coffee and Bikes at the Meteor **18**

16. Be Casual at The Rail: A Pizza Company **19**

17. Finish with a Turkish Coffee at Toot Beirut Shawarma & More **20**

18. Don't Skip Dessert at Tusk & Trotter American Brasserie **21**

19. Catch That Speakeasy Vibe at Undercroft **22**

20. Grab an Extra Napkin at Wright's Barbecue **23**

21. Experience the Soul of Mexico at Yeyo's **24**

Music and Entertainment

22. Join the Party at First Fridays in Downtown Bentonville **28**

23. Enter a Different World at 6th Dimension Virtual Reality **29**

24. Stroll Downtown Rogers during Art on the Bricks **30**

25. Be a Part of the Annual Bentonville Film Festival **31**

26. Relax with a Cigar at Black Crown Social Cigar & Whiskey Lounge... **32**

27. Appreciate the Eclectic at Meteor Guitar Gallery **34**

28. Watch a Parade **35**

29. Celebrate Summer Downtown at the Railyard Live Concert Series..... **36**

30. Get Comfy at Skylight Cinema **37**

31. Keep Up with What's New in Our Area **38**

32. Listen to Classical Piano at the Van Cliburn Concerts **39**

33. See the Newly Renovated Victory Theater **40**

34. Walk Inside Your Local Visitor Center **41**

35. Move to the Music at Walmart AMP (Arkansas Music Pavilion) **42**

36. Have a Drone Deliver to Your Back Yard via Walmart **43**

Sports and Recreation

37. Get Outdoors with 37 North Expeditions **46**

38. Be Cool Underground at War Eagle Cavern **47**

39. Slow Down along the Art Trail at Crystal Bridges **48**

40. Walk with a New Best Friend at Best Friends Pet Resource Center **50**

41. Enjoy the Ride at Bikes, Blues & BBQ Motorcycle Rally **51**

42. Get Gardening Advice at the Benton County Master Gardener Association Plant Sale **52**

43. Bike, Walk, or Camp in Coler Mountain Bike Preserve **54**

44. Walk around the Lake at Lake Atalanta Park **55**

45. Watch Bikes Fly at the Railyard **56**

46. Get in the Swing of Things at the Walmart NWA Championship LPGA Tournament **57**

47. Bike up the First Bikeable Building at Ledger **58**

48. See the Sights at the Run Bentonville Half Marathon **60**

49. Fly Above Bentonville and Rogers from Thaden Field **61**

50. Travel from Bella Vista to Fayetteville on the Razorback Regional Greenway Trail **62**

51. Ride a Bike! **64**

52. Get on a Trail at Hobbs State Park-Conservation Area **66**

53. Choose among Many Options at Osage Park **67**

54. Take Aim at the Quiver Archery **68**

55. Skate or Splash at Lawrence Plaza **69**

Culture and History

56. Walk among Modern Art at Bentonville's 21c Hotel **72**

57. Get Hands-On at the Scott Family Amazeum **73**

58. Buy Original Art from an Art-o-mat® Vending Machine **74**

59. Tour a Frank Lloyd Wright Design at the Bachman-Wilson House **75**

60. Experience the Architecture of E. Fay Jones in Bella Vista **76**

61. Discover a Varied History at Bella Vista Historical Museum **78**

62. Learn about the Early Years at the Bentonville History Museum **79**

63. Learn More about the Public Art in Bentonville **80**

64. Experience These Treasures at Crystal Bridges Museum of American Art **81**

65. Appreciate Nature at Compton Gardens and Arboretum **82**

66. Take a Selfie with the *World's Largest BB Gun* at the Daisy Airgun Museum **84**

67. Discover Bentonville with a Guide with Big on Bentonville Tours **85**

68. Travel through Time at the Museum of Native American History **86**

69. Learn about a Decisive Civil War Battle at Pea Ridge National Military Park **87**

70. See Two Different Homes from the 1800s at the Peel Museum & Botanical Garden **88**

71. Understand What Shaped This Area at the Rogers Historical Museum **89**

72. Immerse Yourself in the Moment at the Momentary **90**

73. Envision a 200-Year-Old Mill at War Eagle Mill **91**

74. Focus on One Part of the Sky Inside James Turrell's Skyspace, *The Way of Color* **92**

75. See Arkansas's First Agri-Hood at Red Barn Farm **94**

76. Volunteer Because So Many Need You **95**

Shopping and Fashion

77. Discover 8th Street Market **98**

78. Discover and Shop in Historic Downtowns **100**

79. Take Your Cooking and Your Kitchen up a Level at Honeycomb Kitchen Shop **101**

80. Walk into the Showroom of A.G. Russell Knives **102**

81. Show Your Loyalty at Bentonville Mercantile and Rogers Mercantile **103**

82. Support Your Local Independent Bookstore **104**

83. Wander Roomfuls of Used Books at the Friendly Bookstore **106**

84. Shop Metaphysical at the Sage Elephant **107**

85. Donate and Shop to Empower Others at Beautiful Lives Thrift Boutique **108**

86. Relax, Dinner Inspiration Can Be Found at Bentonville Provisions **109**

87. Buy Your Puppy a Present at Three Dog Bakery **110**

88. Browse among Beautiful Things at Cobblestone & Vine **112**

89. Find or Make an Everlasting Arrangement at Common Dwellings **113**

90. Shop Local at Downtown Farmers Markets **114**

91. Keep Your Crafting Muse Amused at Hillfolk Textile Studio + Shop **115**

92. Find a Unique Gift at Kaleidoscope Collective **116**

93. Breathe In at the Little Candle of NWA **117**

94. Shop inside a *Fixer to Fabulous* Renovation at Marrs Mercantile **118**

95. Find the Perfect Present at Area Museum Gift Shops **120**

96. Shop Fair-Trade at Remedy Road **122**

97. Fill Your Pantry with Flavor at the House of Webster Gift Shop **123**

98. Create a Charcuterie Board at Sweet Freedom Cheese **124**

99. Browse Local and Regional Arts and Crafts at Wishing Spring Gallery & Gift Shop **126**

100. Save Money, Live Better at Walmart Supercenter Store #0001 .... **128**

Activities by Season **129**

Suggested Itineraries **131**

Index **137**

Mural at 8th Street Market

Maman sculpture from Crystal Bridges Art Trail in Bentonville

INTRODUCTION

Over 150 million tourists visit Northwest Arkansas each year, and about 36 people a day move into this area. Welcome! I hope you each enjoy your time here. The people who arrived before you created an amazing place in a beautiful location.

And to the people who have been here awhile, even those who grew up here, like me: I hope this book will help you discover new things to do and show off an area you love to others.

The more I researched this book, the more excited I got about sharing these destinations with you. My few sentences are an invitation for you to go on a discovery of your own. Get updates on an enticing new place or event on their website, then go explore. If you do that even a few times, that would be wonderful. Write in this book. Put it in your car or on your nightstand. Gift one to a new neighbor or employee. Have a blast exploring Bentonville and Rogers!

Conifer in Bentonville

FOOD AND DRINK

1

DRIVE THROUGH THE VERY FIRST LOCATION

OF 7 BREW

That's right, the first 7 Brew drive-through coffee stand location was in Rogers. With their more than 200 locations and growing, you may be familiar with 7 Brew's coffee drinks, smoothies, teas, and energy drinks served to a continuous line of loyal customers. If you are not familiar, browse the online menu of drinks and dozens of syrups and sauces (many sugar-free) to decide on your order. Don't expect to drive up to a huge sign displaying their menu and prices. I have told one of the friendly folks who work there that I am in the mood for "something with chocolate and caramel," and they were happy to recommend a coffee drink to me. Their secret sauce is a feeling, with a staff that leaves you with a great drink and a smile.

2101 S 52nd St., Rogers
7brew.com

TIP

There are at least a half dozen other 7 Brew locations in Benton County, all serving drinks and smiles.

TAKE A SHOPPING BREAK
AT ARTISAN WOOD FIRED KITCHEN

The first things that catch your eye when you walk in the door of this locally owned restaurant are two huge, wood-fired ovens imported from Italy. Snatch a seat facing the ovens, because watching the ovens and the staff at work is part of the experience. A seat on the patio with a view of the busy Pinnacle Hills Promenade shopping center sidewalks is also a good choice. Artisan Wood Fired Kitchen is perfectly located for a shopping break or a bite before you head to the movies.

Those wood-fired ovens produce an array of creative, delicious pizzas and flatbreads, but calzones, ravioli, pastas, and salads are also on the menu.

The adults will appreciate the well-stocked bar, and children (including your inner child) will delight in the Tableside S'mores Experience, where marshmallows are roasted over an open flame before being placed on graham crackers spread with Nutella.

2203 S Promenade Blvd., Rogers, 479-877-6732
artisanwoodfiredkitchen.com

3

INDULGE
AT BAKED BY KORI

This bakery has rave reviews online—and rightfully so. Their sweet and savory baked goods are rich and flavorful. They are known for cookies, brownies, cake pops, cupcakes, and quiches. They are also a wine bar with a tempting menu. How does a roasted-in-house turkey sandwich on their sourdough bread sound for lunch?

Even better, how 'bout leaving the home office one afternoon and working on your computer with a view of historic downtown buildings, a glass of wine, and a freshly baked brownie? Or quiche and coffee?

Baked by Kori creates made-to-order cakes. I attended a party where one of their vegan cakes was served and everyone raved about how delicious it was. They keep vegan options in the bakery case (unless someone gets excited about finding freshly baked vegan sweets and buys them all!).

128 S 2nd St., Rogers, 479-278-7390
bakedbykori.com

TIP

Baked by Kori may be open before or after a concert or play at the nearby Victory Theater—a winning combination!

4

EXPERIENCE FARM-TO-TABLE FINE DINING
AT CONIFER

Chef Matthew Cooper's imaginative, fresh, gluten-free dishes have made him a James Beard Award Semifinalist, Best Chef South in 2024.

Conifer's Sunday Suppers are a shareable family-style meal. The rest of the week, the dinner menu is not only sustainable but reflects the changing harvests from local farmers. The menu is small and everything on it is exquisite, including the desserts. The gluten-free bread is epic. You have time for a house cocktail while your dinner is being prepared. The chef and staff creating your dinner and the bar are in full view but do not dominate the atmosphere, which is calming and perfect for conversations. Make reservations in advance for this popular restaurant.

321 SE 2nd St., Bentonville, 479-203-5999
coniferbentonville.com

5

THINK ABOUT CRYSTAL BRIDGES AS ANOTHER PLACE FOR COFFEE

AT ELEVEN

Crystal Bridges is a world-class museum, one that people book plane tickets and hotel rooms to see. An area resident or frequent visitor has the freedom to visit Crystal Bridges as often as they like. With free admission and parking, there is no reason you can't think of Eleven, the coffee shop and restaurant inside Crystal Bridges, as another option for Onyx coffee, lunch, or a glass of wine. Did you know Eleven has happy hours?

You can enjoy your coffee in the indoor seating area with views of the spring-fed pond and dramatic architecture. Down a long flight of steps is a waterside patio where you can sit outside.

Stay for a bit to stroll the wooded grounds, view the galleries, or browse the gift shop. Or spend time alone with your thoughts, camera, or sketchbook.

Inside Crystal Bridges Museum of American Art
600 Museum Way, Bentonville
crystalbridges.org/food-and-drink

PLAN A PIZZA NIGHT OUT
AT GUSANO'S CHICAGO-STYLE PIZZERIA

Gusano's serves Chicago-style and traditional pizza, as well as pastas, calzones, sandwiches, wraps, salads, appetizers, beers, wines, and sodas. The owner originally came from Chicago via the University of Arkansas and opened the first Gusano's in Little Rock. Now three of the eight locations are in Benton County: Bentonville, Bella Vista, and Rogers.

Whatever the story, the pizza is great and the atmosphere of this popular family restaurant is casual and welcoming. It is common to see area sports teams of all ages gather at Gusano's after a game or a family with one of the children in a sports uniform. Each location has a different vibe, so try a few to find your favorite.

2905 S Walton Blvd., Ste. 9, Bentonville, 479-271-8242
gusanos.pizza/bentonville

2603 W Pleasant Grove Rd., Ste. 112, Rogers, 479-636-0400
gusanos.pizza/rogers

19 Cunningham Corner, Bella Vista, 479-876-6969
gusanos.pizza/bella-vista

7

TRY A SANDWICH
AT IRON HORSE COFFEE COMPANY

This two-story coffeehouse has been in a historic building in downtown Rogers for over 25 years. I usually order my drink at the counter downstairs and carry it upstairs to a secluded table or sofa to work or sketch. They encourage you to browse and look at the many shelves of books in this coffee shop.

One night a group of us gave up on finding a table at a downtown restaurant and walked into Iron Horse Coffee Company to regroup. I did not realize that they make soups and sandwiches from scratch—or that they also offer sodas and alcoholic beverages. We ordered five different sandwiches and sat at a spacious table. Good background music and a quiet space made conversation easy. Every one of us loved our sandwiches. Now it is on my radar as a downtown lunch option.

220 S 1st St., Rogers, 479-631-9977
ironhorsecoffee.net

8

FEEL AT HOME
IN JACLYN'S KITCHEN

When I mentioned that I was writing this book, everyone who lives near Beaver Lake raved about Jaclyn's Kitchen. This diner has a staff who strike up conversations as they serve delicious food. There is a true sense of community here.

The first big decision to make is whether to have breakfast or lunch. Jaclyn's Kitchen is open early morning to early afternoon, with breakfast served the whole time and lunch served 11 a.m. until 2 p.m. Jaclyn is known for her pancakes, biscuits and gravy, andouille omelet, Reuben, and French dip, but you truly cannot go wrong with anything on the menu. Jaclyn's Kitchen was featured on America's Best Restaurants (americasbestrestaurants.com) in 2024.

In warmer weather, seating on the deck with a view of the woods becomes popular. The lower level serves pizza on summer evenings, with an ice cream stand that is busy. This is a must-try, a quick eight minutes from downtown Rogers.

14438 E Hwy. 12, Rogers, 479-925-7484
jaclynskitchen.net

9

WATCH THE PLANES WHILE HAVING LUNCH
AT LOUISE

In 1936, Bentonville native Louise Thaden and copilot Blanche Noyes flew from Brooklyn to Los Angeles in under 15 hours, setting a new east–west speed record. In 1929, Thaden held the women's altitude, speed, and endurance record simultaneously. Louise is the perfect name for the restaurant inside the Thaden Fieldhouse at the Bentonville Municipal Airport, where tables provide a view of small planes taxiing and parking.

Whether arriving by plane or car, entry into the restaurant is through a hangar, and past the gift shop and exhibits honoring Louise Thaden. You can enjoy a grown-up lunch in the outdoor seating area while the kids (and your inner child) have a fantastic time surrounded by Lake Bentonville, Osage Park, and planes and helicopters taking off and landing.

The history and setting—plus the delicious food—make this a go-to restaurant to take out-of-town guests. Lunch and dinner options are fresh and creative. Their breakfasts are stellar.

2205 SW I St., Ste. 100, Bentonville, 479-250-0477
louise.cafe

TIP

A walk among Osage Park's habitats and outdoor art is convenient and relaxing after a meal. The path is steps away from Thaden Fieldhouse, as are a large playground and benches.

INDULGE IN AWARD-WINNING FRIED CHICKEN
AT MONTE NE INN

Only 10 minutes from Highway 49 or downtown Rogers is a restaurant that has generations of loyal customers. With limited hours and many awards, reservations are needed to make sure there is a table for you.

No need to look at a menu. Everyone enjoys the same meal. After your drinks are ordered and delivered, a kettle of delicious bean soup arrives. That's followed by bowls of fried chicken, mashed potatoes, gravy, green beans, corn, coleslaw, and bread with apple butter. They are happy to refill at this all-you-can-eat restaurant. I highly recommend the blackberry cobbler on the dessert menu, though I doubt you will have room for it. Everything is a set price; drinks and dessert are extra options.

This Beaver Lake restaurant is iconic, unassuming, and well loved. The walls are filled with antiques, conversations are easy to hear, and parking is abundant across the street.

13843 E Hwy. 94, Rogers, 479-636-5511
monteneinnchicken.net

TIP

Fascinating photos and stories about Monte Ne, a resort developed in the early 1900s on land now covered by Beaver Lake, are on exhibit in the Rogers Historical Museum.

11

PICK UP LUNCH, IDEAS, AND INGREDIENTS
AT NOLA'S PANTRY

The foodie couple who opened Nola's Pantry obviously love combining flavors and working with fresh ingredients. Just reading the menu inspires me to try new combinations on my own—and I can. Because in the extensive pantry of spreads, spices, soup mixes, cocktail syrups, and more are some of the ingredients they use. Did you enjoy the sour cherry jam on your turkey sandwich? Take a jar home.

Nola's Pantry is open for breakfast, including many smoothies and coffee drinks. Their more traditional breakfast dishes, salads, and sandwiches have a creative twist with flavors that dance together. The cocktail syrups they sell in the pantry are also used to create mimosas, mocktails, and lemonade, or you can choose beer or wine. Nola's Pantry has seating inside, outdoor dining under cover, and a ride-up order window for bikes off Railyard Loop on First Street.

103 W Chestnut St., Ste. 100, Rogers, 479-278-2432
nolaspantry.com

DRINK BEER, DO GOOD
AT OZARK BEER COMPANY

Ozark Beer Company was founded in 2013 and within five years received numerous awards, including being on the list of *Food & Wine*'s Best IPAs in America, *Southern Living*'s 18 Best Southern Craft Beers, *Men's Journal*'s Top 101 Beers in America (BDCS), and *Paste Magazine*'s 50 Most Underrated Craft Breweries in the USA.

The taproom in downtown Rogers offers pints, growlers, and flights and has a local food truck parked nearby. Their Ozark IPA is very popular, but my favorite is the BDCS—Bourbon Double Cream Stout.

Ozark Beer Company supports businesses and nonprofits in a big way. Drink Beer, Do Good is a daylong event where that month's nonprofit interacts with guests in the taproom and receives $1 from every flight, pint, etc. Other events include the monthly Books and Brews book club with the Rogers Public Library, fun runs like the Underachievers .5K, and art exhibits.

109 N Arkansas St., Rogers, 479-636-2337
ozarkbeercompany.com

13

COZY UP WITH FRESHLY BAKED GOODNESS

AT OLLY MAKES BAKERY

What once was a home in downtown Bentonville is now a bakery well worth discovering. Choose your sweet or savory treat, and find a nook in one of the cozy adjoining rooms to chat with friends or spend a bit a quiet time. The chairs, sofas and decor make you feel like you are in a bed & breakfast or weekending in someone's home.

Whatever is on the menu: cookie, muffin, scone, cake, sausage roll, cupcake . . . rest assured it is gluten-free (yes, everything is gluten-free), free of artificial dyes, and using mainly organic ingredients. Vegan options are noted on the menu, which changes daily and is often posted on the bakery's Instagram feed and website.

The patio outside is another great seating option. With large trees nearby, you feel like you are in an outdoor room with a view of downtown.

220 N Main St., Bentonville, 479-321-2372
ollymakesbakery.com

GO BEYOND THE FAMILIAR
AT BENTONVILLE TACO & TAMALE CO.

With that name in big letters on the brick wall in downtown Bentonville, you know exactly what you're getting into—right? Not quite. Yes, there are tacos and tamales, lots of them. But not the predictable combos. Instead, this restaurant celebrates "Ark-Mex" style with options like made-from-scratch Delta Pulled Pork Tamales. Indulge in Nacho Skillets, one of the cheese dips, or try a fresh salad—they make their dressings daily.

As much as I enjoyed my meal, I must admit the architecture made my heart sing even more. Bentonville Taco & Tamale is in an 1880s bank building. The high ceilings, tile floors, and brick walls that celebrate the past are complemented with lively colors, sleek lines, neon, and large windows. Online, you can reserve the table for six to eight people in the old bank vault.

101 W Central Ave., Bentonville, 479-448-4480
tacoandtamale.com

TIP

Spend an afternoon browsing Bentonville stores before happy hour at Bentonville Taco & Tamale Co. They are open seven days a week, but happy hour is not offered every day.

15

RELAX WITH COFFEE AND BIKES
AT THE METEOR

Part coffee shop, part bottle shop, part bicycle repair and sale, and right on the Razorback Greenway Trail: the Meteor. It has the best cup and saucer (which is for sale there), indoor and outdoor seating, and mellow music and people. It is steps away from the Momentary and near the Bentonville Visitor's Center (with people who have lots of ideas to help you have a great time in Bentonville). Wine tastings happen one night a week, the Worthy Wine Club helps you experience new wines, and a glass of wine or a bottle you buy can be served with your food order (no corkage fee).

The first location of this business (with a memorable motto of "Espresso. Champagne. Chain Lube.") was in Austin, Texas. Then Bentonville. Now there are locations in Dallas and Fayetteville.

401 SE D St., Bentonville, 479-268-4747
themeteor.cafe/bentonville

BE CASUAL
AT THE RAIL: A PIZZA COMPANY

There is nothing fancy about The Rail. That is part of its charm. The Rail has been in one of Rogers's downtown historic buildings near the railroad track for over a decade.

The Rail is relaxed and casual. Nothing artsy on your plate. OK, the wedge salad is pretty special. But really, it's a go-to place to gather, with a good chance of friends running into each other while they are there. There often is a line of people waiting for a table. The wings and pork shanks are well loved. You know you can count on good pizza, beer, and friendly people. And there are many beer and pizza options on the menu, including favorites from local breweries. There is a slice-of-the-day lunch special, and if a train goes by while you are there, you can get a special price on your beer. The outdoor patio is covered and sheltered from wind.

218 S 1st St., Rogers, 479-633-8808
railpizza.com

FINISH WITH A TURKISH COFFEE
AT TOOT BEIRUT SHAWARMA & MORE

Now I know why people get excited when they see Turkish coffee on a menu. Turkish coffee is a perfect end to a delicious meal in this sunny space with a calming landscaped area on the other side of the glass wall.

Toot Beirut Shawarma & More is rated highly and praised for its authentic Mediterranean and Middle Eastern cuisine. The menu includes shawarma, hummus, falafel, and kebobs, plus sandwiches and salads. You may choose to try one of the dinners and platters that serve two or four in the restaurant or to go. Adding a box of handmade sweets will give you hero status when you arrive home.

Awards and articles about Chef Khaled Alkhatib on the wall near the dessert display case (baklava!) will confirm you came to the right place.

5208 Village Pkwy., Ste. 11, Rogers, 479-268-5013

TIP

Talent runs in the family! Sal Alkhatib, Chef Khaled's brother, is also a chef and owner of an excellent Mediterranean restaurant. Aren't we lucky?

Vivace Mediterranean Cuisine
1100 SE 14th St., Bentonville, 479-273-5500

DON'T SKIP DESSERT
AT TUSK & TROTTER AMERICAN BRASSERIE

Tusk & Trotter opened in a much quieter downtown Bentonville the same year Crystal Bridges opened. There have been significant changes in downtown and all of Bentonville in the past decade plus. Tusk & Trotter will be seeing change again when the block it is on transitions to an expansive pedestrian space, making downtown even more vibrant.

The food at Tusk & Trotter is creative, fresh, and flavorful, described as "high South cuisine" and "gourmet comfort food." Whether you are looking for a drink and pub fare after work, lighter salads and flatbreads, or a memorable signature cocktail and entrée, Tusk & Trotter will not disappoint. But, oh my!—do not miss dessert. The Trot on Over is a sticky toffee pudding cake with maple bacon ice cream and espresso sauce. It is even more decadent and delicious than it sounds.

110 SE A St., Bentonville, 479-268-4494
tuskandtrotter.com

TIP

Tusk & Trotter is also known for their weekend brunches.

CATCH THAT SPEAKEASY VIBE
AT UNDERCROFT

The downtown 1904 restored church that houses the Preacher's Son restaurant has a side archway marked "bar" and a basement door marked "coatroom." These doors lead to the warm, dark, comfy cocktail bar that serves select plates from the Preacher's Son's menu.

Find a spot at the bar, slip onto a sofa, or slide into a cozy booth. Ah, you are ready to order a handcrafted cocktail, made at a bar that sets the speakeasy stage for the space. Find out if live music will be playing on a corner stage on their website.

Enjoy dinner in (reservations highly recommended) or at least get a glimpse inside the Preacher's Son restaurant upstairs. The renovated church and the art glass windows created by George Dombek are stunning.

201 NW A St., Bentonville, 479-445-6065
undercroftbar.com

GRAB AN EXTRA NAPKIN
AT WRIGHT'S BARBECUE

Wright's Barbecue started with a food truck before the first restaurant opened. They cook their meats using the method of open flame, 100 percent wood fire, on a pit. Now there are four locations, including Bentonville and Rogers. My favorite location is in downtown Bentonville with a patio overlooking Compton Gardens and the Razorback Greenway. Lunch on the patio, followed by a stroll through Compton Gardens or the nearby Crystal Bridges Art Trail, makes for a perfect afternoon.

Your ribs, sausage, brisket, or combination of meats are served on brown paper on a metal tray, surrounded by your choice of sides: mac and cheese, baked beans, green beans, etc. It is all messy and delicious and perfect. Count on waiting in line—this is a very popular place. They post business hours with the disclaimer "or until we run out of food." We understand.

208 NE 3rd St., Bentonville
5001 W Pauline Whitaker Pkwy., Rogers
479-935-2834
wrightsbbq.com

21

EXPERIENCE THE SOUL OF MEXICO
AT YEYO'S

Yeyo's started with a farm here in Benton County, then a food truck, then a popular restaurant, then a Mezcaleria. Truly a Rios family business, harvests from the farm continue to help create traditional Mexican street fare with a farm-to-table special touch. So special, in fact, that Chef Rafael Rios was named a James Beard Award Semifinalist, Best Chef South in 2020, 2022, 2023, and 2024.

Yeyo's makes their own non-GMO and gluten-free corn tortillas and corn products in-house. The location in 8th Street Market is casual dining; the downtown Rogers location has a different vibe. The downtown Bentonville food truck operates during the warmer months (rumor has it we will see another food truck soon). Menus and inspiring photos are available on their website.

yeyosnwa.com

YEYO'S LOCATIONS

Yeyo's
The main restaurant offers casual dining and a full bar in Bentonville's 8th Street Market.
801 SE 8th St., Ste. 41, Bentonville, 479-657-6954

Yeyo's Mezcaleria y Taqueria
This location's bar has the biggest Mezcal collection in the state. Cultural art decorates the brick walls of the restored modern/rustic 1907 in downtown Rogers.
Inside the 1907, Downtown Rogers
101 E Walnut St., Rogers, 479-372-4700

Yeyo's Yellow Truck, Bentonville Square
This food truck serves Mexican street fare and ice cream from spring through fall in downtown Bentonville.
122 W Central Ave., Bentonville, 479-381-1726

The Victory Theater

MUSIC AND ENTERTAINMENT

22

JOIN THE PARTY
AT FIRST FRIDAYS IN DOWNTOWN BENTONVILLE

Imagine a huge neighborhood block party every month, all summer long. The block is the Bentonville Square, surrounded by restaurants and shops, filled with music and vendors, shaded by mature trees, and welcoming all. That happens on the first Friday of every month, April through October. Now, let's add a theme for every month and boom!—we've got First Friday.

Over 12,000 in our "neighborhood" attended each of these family-friendly gatherings in 2023. Themes centered on art, pets, back to school, and more. Sponsors set up stations and hands-on activities, and photo ops are available.

This truly is a party feel with a relaxed dress code. Just load the family in the car (or on bikes) and head downtown. Festivities start midafternoon, so you can get home before dark or attend later as a date night.

downtownbentonville.org/event/ff

ENTER A DIFFERENT WORLD

AT 6TH DIMENSION VIRTUAL REALITY

6th Dimension Virtual Reality has eight spaces where you can put on VR headpieces and step into another world. For most of the customers, this is a gaming world with zombies and shooting, but there are also options where two people can have a snowball fight or you can bang drums to music to get your Viking crew rowing.

This is a popular place for birthday parties or to keep kids happy while others are shopping at the Pinnacle Hills Promenade. Out-of-town teenage guests? This would be a good option. Younger crowd? Let them beat you at a snowball fight; no one will get hurt. And there are many places for lunch after in Pinnacle Hills Promenade. Go online first to make sure a spot is waiting for you at 6th Dimension Virtual Reality when you get there.

2203 S Promenade Blvd., Rogers
6thdimensionvr.com

TIP

6th Dimension Virtual Reality also does VR repairs (fixmyoculus.com).

STROLL DOWNTOWN ROGERS
DURING ART ON THE BRICKS

Art on the Bricks is a celebration of art from late afternoon into evening on the second Thursday of each month in downtown Rogers. Art galleries and shops offer extended hours and focus on spotlighting local artists and handmade crafts. There may be a reception, a pop-up exhibit, hands-on kids' activities, local artist visits, or classes during this time. You are encouraged to stroll between shops, galleries, and restaurants at this family-friendly event.

Continue your evening with dinner or a drink downtown. You are in the nine-plus-block Railyard Entertainment District, which means drinks served in district cups can go with you as you walk around designated areas and into businesses signed "District Drinks Are Welcome." Find a place to sit in Railyard Park, on a bench, or at a restaurant when you run into a friend. Find more information at rogersar.gov/1411/entertainment-districts.

Downtown Rogers, 479-619-3195
artonthebricks.com

BE A PART
OF THE ANNUAL BENTONVILLE FILM FESTIVAL

The Bentonville Film Festival is chaired by Academy Award winner Geena Davis with Walmart as the founding sponsor. This annual festival is much bigger and more inclusive than I imagined. In fact, inclusivity is how it started over a decade ago. The Bentonville Film Festival champions women and underrepresented voices, including LGBTQIA+, BIPOC, AAPI, and people with disabilities.

More than 150,000 people around the world will be watching at-home screenings in the six competition sections, plus discussion panels.

Inclusivity also means those of us in Northwest Arkansas. Tickets, internships, volunteer opportunities, workshops, and more are available to regional students. Free family movies are shown at the Geena Davis Outdoor Theater during the summer festival. Affordable tickets allow area residents to attend screenings in Bentonville. Local volunteers help make the festival happen.

bentonvillefilm.org/bentonville-film-festival

RELAX WITH A CIGAR
AT BLACK CROWN SOCIAL CIGAR & WHISKEY LOUNGE

Not everyone appreciates a good cigar, which is why a place that not only sells cigars but provides a relaxing spot to appreciate one can be a welcome sight.

As a nonsmoker, I wasn't expecting to have an enjoyable evening at a cigar bar when seven of us gathered at Black Crown Social in downtown Rogers. Seating groups were comfy and purifiers made sure it wasn't too smoky. The bartender at this family business helped two in our group select cigars and whiskey. The rest of us ordered wine and drinks and we all enjoyed a few hours of conversation. The view out the large sliding glass doors onto the Railyard Bike Park with bikes enjoying the lighted park despite the cold evening, must be fun when they open up those doors on warmer evenings.

216 E Poplar St., Rogers, 479-278-7307
blackcrownsocial.com

OTHER CIGAR BARS IN THE AREA

The Cigar District

The cigar store and gift shop in this locally owned business is smoke-free and near the customer lounge. For members, there is an upscale, upstairs lounge with humidified lockers, and a large rooftop patio.

200 SE 6th St., Bentonville, 479-273-7473

thecigardistrict.com

One Eyed Jacks

In business since 2014, this local lounge has a well-stocked bar that includes more than 170 whiskeys. Leather seats inside; more seating outdoors.

2308 SE 28th St., Ste. 12, Bentonville, 479-876-8898

oejcigarlounge.com

27

APPRECIATE THE ECLECTIC
AT METEOR GUITAR GALLERY

Enter the front door of Meteor Guitar Gallery and you'll see a lot of guitars. It is a guitar store with more than a thousand instruments and amplifiers. Any spot not displaying guitars is used to display art. But venture farther . . .

The Meteor Guitar Gallery is in a hundred-year-old, restored movie theater. The owner told me that the historic stage (now with an LED screen backdrop) is the reason why a few movie scenes were filmed inside. The theater holds more than 350 people for musical events and indie films and is one of the venues for the Bentonville Film Festival.

Their website calendar lists music acts performing. The space is also available to rent for private events.

Meteor Guitar Gallery is eclectic, and I love how it, and its historic building facade, adds character to downtown Bentonville.

128 W Central Ave., Bentonville, 479-268-1500
meteorguitargallery.com

WATCH A PARADE

Growing up in Northwest Arkansas, I have seen many small-town parades. Some of you may not believe me, but they are real, not just Hallmark movie scenes or pictures on museum walls. And they are community-filled, with people on the side cheering for friends and family members. The people on the floats probably came together to help create that float. And parents with kids are remembering when they went to that parade with their parents.

Bentonville and Rogers have popular annual Christmas parades. One of the best places for a classic small-town parade is Pea Ridge. Pea Ridge is not just a bedroom community. Families have been here for generations, and people take a moment to chat with the person behind the counter at the bank and the post office. And they have a few parades each year, including Freedom Fest, near the 4th of July.

cityofpearidge.com

29

CELEBRATE SUMMER DOWNTOWN

AT THE RAILYARD LIVE CONCERT SERIES

Railyard Live is a series of live Friday and Saturday night concerts, summer into fall in downtown Rogers. All concerts are free and family friendly. Keep in mind, each guest should register before they go and must show proof of registration to get in.

There is a paved area with reserved tables and chairs (reserve yours quickly because they are popular) or bring your chair or blanket onto the lawn.

You are welcome to bring your own food and nonalcoholic beverages or buy food and drinks from the concessions.

Come early to shop or have dinner downtown. The Downtown Entertainment District allows you to carry designated open containers as you walk around the district and into businesses that participate. Kids may enjoy the splash pad and playground before the concert.

101 E Cherry St., Rogers
railyardlive.com

30

GET COMFY
AT SKYLIGHT CINEMA

Located close to downtown and the Ledger, Skylight Cinema is one of the main locations for the Bentonville Film Festival. Referred to on its website as the "flagship of more to come," Skylight Cinema shows first-run movies from major and independent studios. It also shows sporting events, classic movies, and other cultural events (*The Met: Live*, please!).

The bar and restaurant are set up along a glass wall overlooking downtown, a great place to relax and chat before your movie starts. There is a good variety of items on the menu. My favorite: the citrus chicken tacos. You are welcome to take your food and drinks in, or they will serve you food and drinks while you are sitting in your comfy theater seat.

Don't worry—they have popcorn and sodas too.

350 SW A St., Bentonville, 479-367-7629
skylightcinemas.com

KEEP UP WITH WHAT'S NEW

IN OUR AREA

Did you know that visitbentonville.com has a weekly podcast, *A New American Town*? It can keep you informed about what's new while dozens of past episodes serve as a reference library. Not sure what to expect at the Bentonville Film Festival? Listen to episodes from a year or two ago. Most episodes are 10 to 20 minutes long.

DWTN Now is a well-done, informative, half-hour TV show that is on KFSM and available on downtownbentonville.org.

Bella Vista has a community TV station you can find at youtube.com/@bellavistacommtv.

NWA Daily (nwadaily.com) and The Bentonville Bulletin (bentonvillebulletin.com) e-newsletters include current stories and events. Local newspaper subscriptions and TV station apps can keep you informed.

Start at these websites, where you can sign up for newsletters, download a visitor's guide and maps, look at event calendars, and/or follow their socials:

visitbentonville.com
downtownbentonville.org
destinationrogers.com
godowntownrogers.com
northwestarkansas.org

LISTEN TO CLASSICAL PIANO
AT THE VAN CLIBURN CONCERTS

The Van Cliburn Concert Series season has ticketed classical performances in the Great Hall at Crystal Bridges. The performers in these concerts often play to large audiences around the world and have won international competitions and awards. And yet we can hear them in a more intimate setting.

Soak in the architecture, the view of trees, the lake, and the museum through the glass wall beyond the piano, the very talented classical musician creating magic on the piano . . . and, oh, the piano—the Van Cliburn Concert Grand Piano, a Steinway and Sons that was the home practice instrument of internationally acclaimed pianist Van Cliburn.

To bring this opportunity to students, their tickets are deeply discounted.

Crystal Bridges Museum of American Art
600 Museum Way, Bentonville, 479-418-5700
crystalbridges.org/van-cliburn-concert-series

TIP

Past Van Cliburn concerts are available to stream for free through their website.

SEE THE NEWLY RENOVATED

VICTORY THEATER

On March 13, 2024, I watched Pat Metheny perform the opening concert in the newly renovated Victory Theater. This is the same theater that opened to a full house in 1927 and went through several transformations as a vaudeville and movie theater and more. This is the same theater where I watched movies like *The Love Bug* and *The Sound of Music* as a kid, shopped the used bookstore located there later, and enjoyed Rogers Little Theater productions a few years ago.

Rogers Little Theater is now Arkansas Public Theatre, the only all-volunteer community theater in Northwest Arkansas. The Victory Theater, owned by the City of Rogers, is not only ready for larger musical acts but is also the location of the Rogers Short Film Festival and the long-term home of the Arkansas Public Theatre.

116 S 2nd St., Rogers
thevictorytheater.com, arkansaspublictheatre.org

TIP

Don't forget that there are many restaurant options surrounding this downtown theater.

34

WALK INSIDE
YOUR LOCAL VISITOR CENTER

Have you ever walked into your local visitor center? It is very friendly territory for tourists, residents, and local business owners. Everyone inside a visitor center wants to showcase their community.

There are lots of brochures about destinations and events, but it is the face-to-face conversations that are most valuable. The more your host knows about your interests, the more useful information they can share with you. And since they are familiar with the area, they can share insider tips and help you navigate through construction or traffic to where you want to go. They can also recommend stores (because now they know you have a weakness for antiquing, cooking, or local bookstores) or suggest which restaurant has a great patio to enjoy a perfect day close to your destination.

406 SE 5th St., Ste. 6, Bentonville, 479-271-9153
visitbentonville.com

317 W Walnut St., Rogers, 479-636-1240
destinationrogers.com

MOVE TO THE MUSIC
AT WALMART AMP
(ARKANSAS MUSIC PAVILION)

With an 11,000-person capacity, the Walmart AMP (Arkansas Music Pavilion) is the biggest stage house in Arkansas and listed by pollstar.com as one of the Top 100 Amphitheater venues in the world. They continue to offer an impressive schedule of performers—41 shows and events in 2023. General admission seating is on the sloping lawn at this outdoor amphitheater, and 3,200 seats are covered. Now that it has been here for a decade, the Walmart AMP is a familiar part of the skyline in the popular Pinnacle Hills area.

Walmart AMP is a part of the Walton Arts Center in Fayetteville, which brings touring Broadway shows to Northwest Arkansas. The two facilities complement each other rather than compete, leaving us with the best of both worlds. New concerts are announced often, so it pays to follow Walmart AMP on social media.

5079 W Northgate Rd., Rogers, 479-443-5600
amptickets.com

36

HAVE A DRONE DELIVER TO YOUR BACK YARD

VIA WALMART

Of course, Walmart tries out new ideas in the stores near their headquarters. One is drone delivery. Different styles of drones fly from different area stores. Rarely am I in my subdivision backyard for any length of time without a drone flying overhead. By the beginning of 2024, Walmart drone delivery was operating in 36 stores across seven states, with more than 10,000 successful deliveries. Walmart drone delivery is now expanding to the Dallas–Fort Worth area.

Drone delivery comes in handy if you are not feeling well and want cold medication delivered to you or need something while your child is napping. Drone delivery can also be a fun surprise while you have out-of-town guests visiting, certain to impress that eight-year-old when cookies arrive by drone.

walmart.com/cp/drone-delivery/3585490

Razorback Regional Greenway Trail

SPORTS AND RECREATION

GET OUTDOORS
WITH 37 NORTH EXPEDITIONS

Do you want to explore the Ozarks but none of your friends are available or up for it? Do you want to try paddleboarding, kayaking, horseback riding, rock climbing, or camping, but with guidance? Do you need to plan something fun to do when your brother and his family of five visit? Are you in charge of planning a team retreat?

There are many options on 37northexpeditions.com, including private, full- and half-day excursions for two to 11 people. They also have planned full- and half-day opportunities that you can join. Just meet them in Bentonville and they will take care of everything from there. After trying one excursion, you may be ready to sign up for one of their multiday or multisport adventures, overnight retreats, or international trips.

417-501-5455
37northexpeditions.com

BE COOL UNDERGROUND
AT WAR EAGLE CAVERN

Start your visit to War Eagle Cavern through the gift shop, which has a strong focus on stones, and the ticketing counter. There's also gemstone panning, the Lost in the Woods Maze, and the Moonshiners Mystery Shack at the top of the hill to experience. The tour is an enjoyable, easy, lengthy walk down the hill.

The photogenic entry to the cave is on a large bluff near a wooded inlet of Beaver Lake. It is one of the largest cave entrances in Arkansas. As you step inside, you can feel the welcoming, constant 58-degree temperature. Inside, there are cave openings you can stand under and look straight up. There is also a stream within the cave.

Tour guides are knowledgeable and friendly, telling you about the bats, indigenous people, moonshiners, and outlaws that have been in that cave; the geology; and the natural area surrounding the cave (ask about the Ozark chinquapin tree).

21494 Cavern Dr., Rogers, 479-789-2909
wareaglecavern.com

TIP

The 1994 movie *Frank and Jesse* includes scenes filmed inside War Eagle Cavern.

SLOW DOWN ALONG THE ART TRAIL AT CRYSTAL BRIDGES

Follow the Razorback Greenway north from downtown Bentonville (near the Third Street entrance into Compton Gardens) and soon you will see the half-mile Art Trail leading to the south entrance of Crystal Bridges Museum of American Art. Immediately to your right is James Turell's Skyspace, *The Way of Color*.

This wide, paved walk passes by many more sculptures with informative signage until you see *Maman*, a giant metal spider, then more sculptures around the Crystal Bridges south plaza.

Just as inspiring is the setting: an Arkansas forest and stream enhanced by native plantings of Arkansas amsonia, oakleaf hydrangea, and more. At one point you are invited to leave the paved path down stone steps to the stream and a small waterfall. If this natural setting inspires you, there are over five miles of paths on the 120 acres of Crystal Bridges' grounds. Inside the museum are trail maps, restrooms, and coffee.

crystalbridges.org/nature-trails/#trails

TIP

One of the free drop-in tours offered at the Crystal Bridges Museum of American Art is the Sculpture and Nature tour—March through November, weather permitting. Check their website to confirm days and hours this tour is offered.

crystalbridges.org/calendar/drop-in-tour-sculpture-nature

WALK WITH A NEW BEST FRIEND

AT BEST FRIENDS PET RESOURCE CENTER

Best Friends Animal Sanctuary, based in Utah, opened its largest, satellite no-kill shelter in Bentonville in 2023. This shelter uses its vans to bring in animals from full-capacity shelters and invites area shelters to show adoptable animals on weekends. They have an impressive number of adoptions through this shelter.

Looking for a very different coffee shop? Order a drink from Third Space Coffee's vegan menu and sit facing a large window where you can interact with the kittens. Prefer to bring your computer and work? Fine, but you deserve a relaxing break in the cat or kitten room.

The dogs live and play downstairs, but some enjoy being in pens in the atrium. Of course they are looking for forever homes, but people also drop by to visit the animals and check out a dog for the day. Yes, you can borrow a dog to go for a walk with you.

1312 Melissa Dr., Bentonville, 479-310-8569
bestfriends.org/northwest-arkansas

ENJOY THE RIDE
AT BIKES, BLUES & BBQ MOTORCYCLE RALLY

I've always thought of Bikes, Blues & BBQ motorcycle rally like a college football weekend—be aware that the traffic on the roads will increase dramatically on that fall weekend. This gathering of 275,000-plus people in Northwest Arkansas has been happening for over 20 years. Of course, this four-day charity event is a boom to our local economy. Did you know it also has raised over $3 million for more than two dozen local charities?

Bikes, Blues & BBQ moved from Fayetteville to Rogers in 2022. With a dozen suggested rides noting time and difficulty, motorcyclists travel scenic routes that take them from Van Buren to Eureka Springs and into Missouri. Arriving from all 50 states and other countries, participants gather at scheduled events throughout the area, plus area restaurants and motorcycle shops.

479-527-9993
bikesbluesandbbq.org

42

GET GARDENING ADVICE
AT THE BENTON COUNTY MASTER GARDENER ASSOCIATION PLANT SALE

Imagine walking through thousands of plants with dozens of Master Gardeners to help you decide which plants to take home. This happens every May in Benton County.

To help them help you and to stay focused, know what you are looking for. If your garden is a shady woodland, head straight to the shade-loving plants. It also helps to have photos: A picture really is worth a thousand words when trying to describe your garden. You can take photos of informative plant signs and research on your own with your phone.

If you have a folding wagon, put it in your car. There will be wagons there, but at peak times you may have to wait for one.

facebook.com/bentoncountymastergardeners

TIP

Master Gardeners not only help you choose plants, but they also have area beautification projects (funded by plant sale proceeds), a demonstration garden that donates fresh produce, and educational programs. They fund scholarships, too. Becoming a Master Gardener and volunteering beside fellow Master Gardeners helps our community, builds strong friendships, and is an opportunity to be a better gardener.

43

BIKE, WALK, OR CAMP
IN COLER MOUNTAIN BIKE PRESERVE

Coler Mountain Bike Preserve has over 19 miles of mountain bike trails ranging from beginners to very challenging. It is also where I took a beginners' mountain bike class.

But you don't have to have a bike to enjoy Coler. The two-and-a-half-mile paved Applegate Trail runs from Southwest Eighth Street to Northwest Third Street and then north through Coler Park to Peach Orchard Road. It is a popular trail for a run or walk. Although Coler is very close to downtown Bentonville, the natural setting feels miles away.

Coler also has 16 hike-in camping sites, five camper van sites, and one ADA site. You can take the kids camping a few miles from home, where there is an Airship coffee shop (without Wi-Fi, but with highly rated nachos), heated showers, and a mature forest—a weekend minivacation.

Coler Grove parking lot
2500 NW Grove Ln., off NW 3rd St., Bentonville, 479-364-0168
Another parking lot is across 3rd Street.

North lot
11840–11850 Peach Orchard Rd.

peelcompton.org/visit-coler

Camping
peelcompton.org/coler-mountain-bike-preserve/camping

44

WALK AROUND THE LAKE
AT LAKE ATALANTA PARK

Lake Atalanta was a 1930s Works Progress Administration (WPA) project. In the 1960s and '70s, Lake Atalanta had a rectangular swimming pool, a roller rink, and miniature golf that attracted the kids. What emerged after the 2016 renovations is stunning, relaxing, and fun.

A wide, paved path edges the perimeter of the lake now, with several fishing piers jutting into the lake. Dogs on leashes are welcome to walk with you on the wide path around the small lake. There is always a nice view of the surrounding woods, especially when the trees turn colors in autumn.

The park includes five pavilions and three playgrounds, plus a tree house. If that seems too active for you, you can escape into a grove of walnut trees or the serenity garden.

The 236-acre Lake Atalanta includes Railyard Park near downtown. See the next entry.

500 E Walnut St., Rogers, 479-631-3350
rogersar.gov/facilities/facility/details/lake-atalanta-park-15

WATCH BIKES FLY
AT THE RAILYARD

The Railyard is a world-class bike skills park, with bike trails at four levels of difficulty: novice, beginner, intermediate, and expert. One trail goes through an old boxcar with murals, a fun interpretation of the historic Frisco train tracks.

This park is open from early morning until 10 p.m., thanks to recently installed lights. Loved by the local bike community, the Railyard is a tourist destination for many who have seen videos on YouTube and must try it out for themselves. The most amazing part of this park is the people on bikes, who create impressive performances.

The Railyard is considered part of Lake Atalanta Park. Bike paths stretch from the Railyard downtown to Lake Atalanta and into the wooded hillside.

299 E Cherry St., Rogers, 479-631-3350
rogersar.gov/facilities/facility/details/the-railyard-57

GET IN THE SWING OF THINGS AT THE WALMART NWA CHAMPIONSHIP LPGA TOURNAMENT

After 16 years at the Pinnacle Country Club, the Walmart NWA Championship LPGA Tournament is a weeklong, annual celebration in Rogers. The three-day, 54-hole tournament has a $3 million purse and surprisingly affordable tickets. Several volunteer positions are available each year to make this event a success.

The Walmart NWA Championship LPGA Tournament, usually held in late September, has grown to include many supporting events. The 5k @ the LPGA and a 1K Fun Run both support local charities. A special ticket can get you into the Bite Experience @ the LPGA, where you can view the golfing while enjoying foods from several local restaurants. Yoga classes are another option.

For younger people, the Fassi's Friends Junior Clinic offers inclusive and adaptable clinics to include all. There is also a special kids' area at the tournament.

Pinnacle Country Club, Rogers, 479-715-6100
nwachampionship.com

BIKE UP THE FIRST BIKEABLE BUILDING
AT LEDGER

Ledger could fit into many of the categories in this book. This building is truly an extension of the Bentonville community: innovation, bikes, art, coffee, inclusivity.

Ledger is the world's first bikeable building, six floors with 12-foot-wide exterior switchbacks. The public is invited onto the ramp and into the ground floor, with commercial space and the Airship coffee shop.

The steel art tree in the center of the coffee shop is one of many permanent pieces of art on the first level, placed among an abundance of seating, meeting spaces, and phone booths.

The higher floors have a variety of office space. With a daily pass you can plug into a hot desk and focus on your work. Monthly shared space passes, plus short- and long-term office space leases, are available. Each of the 32 meeting rooms permanently displays works by a regional artist. The top members' floor includes a large event space, showers, patio, and a bar.

240 S Main St., Bentonville, 479-579-9644
ledgerbentonville.com

TIP

Notice the many insects carrying gems up the ramp? Take the time to view the wall display on the ground floor of the Ledger building to learn about this artwork by New York–based artist Stefan Sagmeister.

SEE THE SIGHTS
AT THE RUN BENTONVILLE HALF MARATHON

Want to get to know Bentonville better? The Run Bentonville Half Marathon starts at Bentonville Square and takes you through neighborhoods and eight parks, plus by Crystal Bridges Museum of American Art, the Momentary, interesting architecture, public art, and much more. The run has been presented by Bentonville Parks and Recreation for well over a decade, benefitting their parks and programming.

If 13.1 miles and the elevation change shown on the course map cause you to hesitate, share the race with a friend with the Half Marathon Relay or sign up for the 5K. There also is a two-mile nighttime Glow Run later in the spring. That and other runs in the Run Bentonville Race Series can be found on the runbentonville.com website.

Bentonville, 479-464-7275
runbentonville.com/half-marathon

FLY ABOVE BENTONVILLE AND ROGERS
FROM THADEN FIELD

Have you ever wondered what it would be like to fly one of the small planes that are often seen above Bentonville and Rogers? Would you like to see Beaver Lake or your hometown from the sky? From Bentonville Municipal Airport's Thaden Field, 10 minutes from downtown Bentonville, you can schedule one of two different 30-minute flights. One would allow up to three people to enjoy a scenic flight of the area. Another would let you take a discovery flight—where you would be the copilot of a small plane and feel what it is like to take the controls.

If this is an experience you have been dreaming of, you can do that in Bentonville. Just check their website for prices and scheduling information. It is an investment of time and money, but investing in your dreams has a great ROI, don't you think?

2205 SW I St., Bentonville, 479-254-0817
fbo.thadenfield.com/scenic-flights
fbo.thadenfield.com/discovery-flights

TIP

Thaden Fieldhouse has an aviation-themed gift shop and exhibits about Louise Thaden.

TRAVEL FROM BELLA VISTA TO FAYETTEVILLE ON THE RAZORBACK REGIONAL GREENWAY TRAIL

The Razorback Regional Greenway Trail (RRGT) was designated a National Recreation Trail in 2023, adding its nearly 46 miles to the National Trails System. The RRGT is not one trail but a network of more than 20 connecting trails that travel through nine municipalities, including both Bentonville and Rogers. Dozens of parking areas are located near the trails. Many other trails link into the RRGT, making it possible for many people to commute to work on a bike or for a family to bike to dinner on a summer evening.

Whether traveling on shoes, bike, wheelchair, stroller, or whatever, the RRGT can take you to restaurants, museums, parks, natural areas, shopping, and more. It's more than recreation—it is a connector that links two dozen schools (including the University of Arkansas campus), three hospitals, and area corporate headquarters.

razorbackgreenway.org

TIP

Join the party at the spring and fall Square 2 Square Bike Ride. Participants bike from Bentonville to Fayetteville (or the other way; the direction rotates), with pit stops and shuttle services.

razorbackgreenway.org/square-2-square

RIDE A BIKE!

Bentonville is the "Mountain Biking Capital of the World" and the official "Home of the US National Mountain Bike Team." It is also home to many stores, people, and organizations who are happy to help you discover mountain biking and the amazing quantity and variety of area bike trails and facilities. Bike rentals, advice, and classes abound for those wanting to try mountain biking—or any kind of biking.

A good part of the area population owns bikes and many vacation here for the extensive and well-made and maintained bike trails. NorthWest Arkansas Community College offers Trail Technician and Bicycle Assembly & Repair Technician programs—useful skills with over 400 miles of trails in Northwest Arkansas.

TO LEARN ABOUT AREA TRAILS SYSTEMS AND ALL THINGS BIKE, HERE ARE A FEW PLACES TO START.

OZ Trails
Bike trails and resources in Northwest Arkansas.
oztrails.com

Bike Bentonville
All things bike in the Mountain Bike Capital of the World.
visitbentonville.com/bike

Bike Bella Vista
Trails through Bella Vista's natural areas and various terrain.
discoverbellavistaar.com/ride

Women of OZ
A nonprofit bike club with classes, rides, and an annual summit.
woznwa.com

Bentonville Ride Club
Events and group rides.
bentonvillerideclub.com

Maps and videos of Rogers's trail system
rogersar.gov/208/trails-greenways

You can also chat with someone working at any of the many area bike shops.

GET ON A TRAIL
AT HOBBS STATE PARK-CONSERVATION AREA

Start your visit to Hobbs State Park-Conservation Area at the LEED-certified Visitor Center, surrounded by natural landscape and filled with information about the landscape, animals, plants, lake, history, and more. It also has a gift shop any curious kid would love. And the best part is the opportunity to learn more about all of that. Their socials or mailing list can keep you updated on events, talks, walks, boat rides, animal interactions, and more. This park's staff and volunteers are happy to share their expertise and enthusiasm.

Close to the Visitor Center is an accessible Ozark Plateau Trail with informative panels, perfect for strollers and wheelchairs. With over 12,000 acres, Hobbs State Park is Arkansas's largest state park. There's room for 54 miles of trails, including hiking trails, mountain bike trails, and horseback riding trails. Six of their 11 primitive campsites are only accessible by trail.

20201 E Hwy. 12, Rogers, 479-789-5000
arkansasstateparks.com/parks/hobbs-state-park-conservation-area

53

CHOOSE AMONG MANY OPTIONS
AT OSAGE PARK

Osage Park is an urban park with many options and personalities. One area has food trucks, seating under a pavilion, and pickleball courts. From there you can follow the level walking/biking trails through prairie and wetlands, with informative signage about conservation. Meander past benches and public art and you are near a wooded area beside Lake Bentonville, or to a large, popular playground near Thaden Fieldhouse. A large dog park and the Quiver archery range are part of this park.

You will see people fishing at the lake or chatting on a bench, a family riding bikes, a photographer taking advantage of the light at sunset, and lots of people going for walks. You will also see small planes or a helicopter overhead as they are landing at Thaden Field.

And all this magic is happening 10 minutes from downtown Bentonville.

Parking at 700 SW 16th St., Bentonville
peelcompton.org/visit-osage-park

TAKE AIM
AT THE QUIVER ARCHERY

There is a low learning curve on archery and many certified instructors at The Quiver, a world-class archery range. This facility has several archery lanes that you can rent by the hour, with equipment rental included in the fee. A seating area behind the archers lets you sit and chat until it is your turn if you come with friends. Everyone is safe and in sync, and staff are always there to help. This is great family time; ages 8 and older are welcome to shoot on the range.

A membership comes with perks, like cooler morning hours, league play, and a supportive community.

The Quiver Archery is a part of Osage Park, with a separate entrance and parking area but connected by trails to the rest of the park.

1701 SW F St., Bentonville
thequiverarchery.com

55

SKATE OR SPLASH
AT LAWRENCE PLAZA

Lawrence Plaza is a 7,000-square-foot facility that changes with the seasons. It is downtown, between 21c Hotel and Compton Gardens in downtown Bentonville.

During summer months (May through September), it is the Fountains at Lawrence Plaza, a popular splash pad. This is a great spot for families, with lots of benches and interactive art. Evening hours allow for relaxing family time after work and fun lighting. There is a building with restrooms and many options for food, coffee, and ice cream in the area.

During winter (November through February), it becomes the Rink at Lawrence Plaza, a permanent outdoor ice rink. A low admission includes skate rentals, and skating lessons are available. Holiday lighting creates a festive feel.

Year-round, Bentonville Parks and Recreation events also happen here, such as movies and magic shows.

214 NE A St., Bentonville, 479-271-3390
bentonvillear.com/1320/lawrence-plaza

Rogers Historical Museum

CULTURE AND HISTORY

WALK AMONG MODERN ART
AT BENTONVILLE'S 21C HOTEL

Bentonville's 21c Museum Hotel is the second of what is now eight hotels. The name celebrates the 21st-century artwork throughout and outside the building.

Although the eight locations of 21c are defined as art exhibit space with many locations, each a blend of hotel and museum, some of the art is commissioned for a specific location. For example, Monica Mahoney's *Making Change* is the sculpture created from a 1962 Fleetwood Cadillac (the same year the first Walmart store opened). The idea to cover the car with coins started with Walton's Five and Dime on the Bentonville Square. Nickels, dimes, and pennies create a barcode design on the hood and the 21c logo on the roof.

The 12,000-square-foot, inside and outdoor, permanent and rotating art exhibits in the lobby and public spaces of 21c are open to the public. Enjoy a drink among art at the Hive.

200 NE A St., Bentonville, 479-286-6500
21cmuseumhotels.com/bentonville

GET HANDS-ON
AT THE SCOTT FAMILY AMAZEUM

Hands-on, interactive learning in the arts and sciences in the most fun way—that's Amazeum. Creative play for preschool to after school to summer camps fills 50,000 square feet, plus an acre of outdoor space.

Don't think it's only kids who get to play—the fun adults are exploring and pushing buttons and role-playing with them. And you can bet they are going into that Hershey's Lab or finding a babysitter to attend one of their Adult Nights.

This museum does charge an admission, but with family memberships you can go as often as you want, plus there are more benefits worth looking into. There is also one "Priceless Night" a week to make sure everyone can experience Amazeum. Planning a visit? Expected school field trips are on the website, so you have an idea on how crowded it may be.

1009 Museum Way (J Street and Museum Way), Bentonville, 479-696-9280
amazeum.org

TIP

Save the Nature Valley Water Amazements experience for last because it's hard to stay dry when you are having that much fun learning about water. Maybe stash a dry T-shirt in your tote, too.

BUY ORIGINAL ART
FROM AN ART-O-MAT® VENDING MACHINE

An artist having an exhibit decided to convert an old cigarette vending machine to sell his photos at an art show in a North Carolina café. It was such a big hit that the café did not want him to remove the machine. He turned to other artists to help stock the machine and now there are more than 200 Art-o-mat® machines worldwide. The machines themselves are works of art, and the original art inside is—you guessed it—the size of a cigarette box or fits inside of a box that size.

The art is often on wooden blocks that can sit on a shelf. Viewing through the glass, you choose what you want, pull the lever, and—presto! You own an original work of art. You are an art collector.

The Momentary gift shop
507 SE E St., Bentonville, 479-367-7500
themomentary.org
artomat.org

TOUR A FRANK LLOYD WRIGHT DESIGN
AT THE BACHMAN-WILSON HOUSE

Threatened by flooding, the 1950s Bachman-Wilson House was relocated from the banks of the Millstone River in New Jersey to a site overlooking Crystal Spring in a wooded area at Crystal Bridges Museum of American Art in 2015. It is the only Frank Lloyd Wright–designed building in Arkansas.

Built five years before Wright's death, it is an example of classic Usonian architecture meant to bring a new American style to the middle class. Usonian cost-saving materials (such as concrete block walls and concrete floors) and an open floor plan can be seen in the Bachman-Wilson House.

Self-guided tours are free, but it is wise to secure a time slot online before you head to the museum. A guided tour led by someone to tell the history, point out details, and answer questions is well worth the fee.

Crystal Bridges Museum of American Art
600 Museum Way, Bentonville, 479-418-5700
crystalbridges.org/architecture/frank-lloyd-wright-bachman-wilson-house

TIP

Audio tours, virtual tours, and blog posts about the Bachman-Wilson House are available on the Crystal Bridges website.

EXPERIENCE THE ARCHITECTURE OF E. FAY JONES

IN BELLA VISTA

Did you know an area architect received the AIA Gold Medal, the American Institute of Architects' highest honor? Two of his buildings are open to the public in Bella Vista, as is Thorncrown Chapel in nearby Eureka Springs.

The Bella Vista Museum has a nice exhibit on Fay Jones (1921–2004), who was the dean of the University of Arkansas School of Architecture and a friend of Frank Lloyd Wright.

Jones designed the Mildred B. Cooper Chapel on Lake Norwood in Bella Vista. The intricate, delicate chapel is much taller than it is wide. Light and shadow play in the glass and wood arches surrounded by trees, a man-made cathedral within nature's cathedral.

Another of Fay Jones's creations is the Bella Vista Country Club. You can admire the architecture while enjoying lunch, happy hour, or dinner at BV Bar & Grill inside the club.

Mildred B. Cooper Memorial Chapel
504 Memorial Dr., Bella Vista
479-855-6598
cooperchapel.com

BV Bar & Grill in the Bella Vista Country Club
98 Clubhouse Dr., Bella Vista
479-855-5117
bvbarandgrill.com

TIP

A digital exhibit on the influence of Frank Lloyd Wright on Fay Jones's work and a digital brochure on area works by Fay Jones are available on the Crystal Bridges Museum of American Art website.

crystalbridges.org/architecture/frank-lloyd-wright-bachman-wilson-house

DISCOVER A VARIED HISTORY AT BELLA VISTA HISTORICAL MUSEUM

In an area rich in museums, why visit the Bella Vista Historical Museum? Bella Vista has a very different history than Bentonville and Rogers. In 1915, it was planned as a resort with a lake and 400 lots for people farther south escaping brutal summers. Later it became a place to buy vacation homes and retirement homes. Bella Vista made the shift from Arkansas's largest unincorporated community to a city in 2007 and is known as an affordable bedroom community rich in golf courses, nature, and an ever-growing network of trails.

This small museum has impressive, informative exhibits. Did you know that when Louise Thaden flew home to Bentonville with her new pilot's certificate in 1928 there was not an area landing field, so she landed on a golf course in Bella Vista? In 1930 ARKOMA Airways advertised flights from the Bella Vista Airport to Dallas, Kansas City, and other cities.

1885 Bella Vista Way, Bella Vista, 479-855-2335
bellavistamuseum.org

62

LEARN ABOUT THE EARLY YEARS
AT THE BENTONVILLE HISTORY MUSEUM

This museum, located in the old train depot, is new and small, but it's filled with information about Bentonville. This 501(c)(3) nonprofit organization's belief is stated as "Small but Fabulous."

I joined the museum's Bentonville History Walking Tour last year on a Saturday morning. With an engaging guide, and interesting stories, the tour ended in the downtown farmers market. I still had time to buy a few veggies—best of both.

You can also have the best of two worlds with a visit to the Bentonville Museum—seeing what built this small town (apples were a big business before Sam and Helen Walton moved here) and the Frisco caboose beside the building. Then walk across the street to another "Small but Fabulous" place: the 211 Cafe within the Bentonville Library. It's a must-try—the locally roasted coffee beans, grown by friends of the owner, and the chocolate are from Guatemala.

416 S Main St., Bentonville, 479-696-4210
bentonvillehistorymuseum.org

63

LEARN MORE ABOUT THE PUBLIC ART
IN BENTONVILLE

The City of Bentonville website (bentonvillear.com) includes a map locating more than 35 pieces of art on public property. That is impressive, and yet it is far from all the outdoor art displayed for public viewing. Bentonville property does not include the walls and plazas of most buildings, Coler Park, Osage Park, and Compton Gardens. Art is an intrinsic part of Bentonville, available to all residents and visitors.

At the Visit Bentonville website (visitbentonville.com/things-to-do/arts-culture), photos of more than 140 works of art are accompanied by the location, title, artist, and often a narrative about the art. A New Year's resolution to really look at or take a selfie in front of one work of public art each week would not even cover half the art available to you in Bentonville.

The weekly drop-in Sculpture and Nature Tour offered by Crystal Bridges is free and an easy walk, a perfect introduction to outdoor art.

visitbentonville.com/things-to-do/arts-culture

64

EXPERIENCE THESE TREASURES

AT CRYSTAL BRIDGES MUSEUM OF AMERICAN ART

You already know Crystal Bridges Museum of American Art is a world-class museum on 120 acres and well worth visiting. Here are a few personal recommendations:

The free docent-led tours of the collections, architecture, and outdoor sculptures are a great way to learn. Tours of the Frank Lloyd Wright–designed Bachman-Wilson House do cost a fee. Admission to the house is free but limited. Register online to secure a spot for any of these.

A favorite hidden outdoor spot is Arkansas Quartz Crystals near the South Entrance: a grotto created by boulders covered in natural quartz crystals excavated from west-central Arkansas. I love crystals, but I did not know stones made up of hundreds of them even existed. Arkansas has some of the largest and most transparent quartz crystals in the world.

Crystal Bridges events, talks, and classes are stellar. Become a member, get on their email list, or follow their socials to stay informed.

600 Museum Way, Bentonville, 479-418-5700
crystalbridges.org

APPRECIATE NATURE
AT COMPTON GARDENS AND ARBORETUM

Compton Gardens is filled with native perennials, shrubs, and specimen trees—including five State Champion Trees. The main building, once the home of Dr. Neil Compton, includes an exhibit room of his life and contributions.

Dr. Compton was key in organizing the protection of Arkansas's Buffalo River from the construction of dams in the 1960s and helping it become the first designated "National River" in the National Park System.

Part of what makes this six-acre property special is that after a half century of celebrating nature as a private residence it now adjoins Crystal Bridges, the Razorback Greenway, bike trails, a historic neighborhood, and downtown Bentonville. Together, these weave a magical tapestry threading from downtown Bentonville to Crystal Bridges, from Fayetteville to Bella Vista, from woodlands and streams to both historic and modern architecture. Compton Gardens, open sunup to sundown, manages to be both calming and an active community hub at the same time.

312 N Main St., Bentonville, 479-254-3870
peelcompton.org/visit-compton-gardens

TIP

The Compton home also serves as a meeting center where you can rent one room or the center for a retreat, wedding, or party.

TAKE A SELFIE WITH THE *WORLD'S LARGEST BB GUN* AT THE DAISY AIRGUN MUSEUM

Take a selfie in front of the *World's Largest BB Gun*, a 25-foot sculpture propped against the historic downtown building that houses the Daisy Airgun Museum. Much of the Daisy memorabilia and products were collected by, then donated by, Daisy employees to this nonprofit museum. The chronological displays date back to Plymouth Iron Windmill Company in Michigan, which offered a free air rifle to farmers buying a windmill in the 1880s.

Many people are familiar with Daisy's Red Ryder BB gun as the star of *A Christmas Story*. The movie debuted here in Rogers to a small audience of Daisy employees back in 1983—over 40 years ago. There is a display dedicated to the movie, including the leg lamp. Another display focuses on Red Ryder—a comic strip, comic book, radio, TV, and movie character that was introduced around 1940.

202 W Walnut St., Rogers, 479-986-6873
daisymuseum.com

67

DISCOVER BENTONVILLE WITH A GUIDE

WITH BIG ON BENTONVILLE TOURS

This family-owned tour company offers a variety of tours, including the Big on Bentonville Golf Cart Tour, either private or shared.

On the shared 90-minute golf cart tour, you save money and meet new people. Questions will be asked that you may not think of. We were told about history, trends, restaurants, and Bentonville destinations. On the tour I joined there was one couple who loved the HGTV series *Fixer to Fabulous*, so the guide pointed out homes on the show. Another couple lived a few hours away, looking for weekend road trips, so our guide recommended things to do in the area.

Big on Bentonville also offers electric bike tours, supplying e-bikes and helmets and staying on paved streets and trails. By traveling on trails, you access works of art that a golf cart cannot, travel though Arkansas woodlands and over streams, and see a few of the destinations in this book.

479-445-6700
bigonbentonville.com

TRAVEL THROUGH TIME
AT THE MUSEUM OF NATIVE AMERICAN HISTORY

Step into the Museum of Native American History (MONAH) and you are instantly looking at the skeleton of a woolly mammoth from about 12,000 years ago. The exhibits take you chronologically through six periods of time and include tools, sculptures, and clothing.

A few things surprised me about the MONAH. First, this museum is over 16 years old, originally started as a private collection that opened to the public in a downtown Bentonville space in 2008. Second, this collection is of Native Americans in North, Central, and South America. Of course, there are exhibits of artifacts found in Arkansas, but being able to see the similarities and differences of items throughout the Americas enriches the experience. Third, the number of items on exhibit is impressive, as is the website, which includes recorded presentations and detailed descriptions of collection pieces in their artifact blog.

The gift shop includes contemporary jewelry, art, and more made by Native American artists.

202 SW O St., Bentonville, 479-273-2456
monah.org

LEARN ABOUT A DECISIVE CIVIL WAR BATTLE
AT PEA RIDGE NATIONAL MILITARY PARK

Pea Ridge is the location of the most decisive battle of the Civil War west of the Mississippi River. Imagine 16,000 Confederate soldiers marching north 60 miles in three winter days with two days' rations and one blanket each. The 13,000 who survived the journey fought 10,000 Union soldiers at the two-day Battle of Pea Ridge, the most decisive Civil War battle west of the Mississippi River. The theater and museum in the Visitor Center tell the story in detail.

What surrounds the Visitor Center is the 4,400-acre battlefield with a seven-mile, 10-stop tour road. Overlooks not only tell the story but also show off the geography of this area. Want to walk or ride your bike on paved roads? The grounds are open basically sunrise to sunset, seven days a week. Check the website for information about this park located 10 miles north of Rogers, just off US Highway 62.

15930 National Park Dr., Garfield, 479-451-8122
nps.gov/peri/index.htm

SEE TWO DIFFERENT HOMES FROM THE 1800S

AT THE PEEL MUSEUM & BOTANICAL GARDEN

Colonel Samuel West Peel, the first native Arkansan elected to the United States Congress, had this house built from local bricks shortly after the Civil War. The free tour represents this family's life in the late 1800s.

One of the Peels' nine children was married in the parlor in 1891. One hundred years later, the newly formed Peel House Foundation acquired the house and created the house museum through restoration and furnishings (some loaned from other museums).

The entry and gift shop are in an antebellum log cabin moved from another part of the county, offering a glimpse of life from another time and social status. The gardens are laid out to be a continuous discovery and delight. In the summer, paths lead from a vibrant riot of blooms covered with butterflies and bees to the shade of a majestic tree to a secluded garden with a fountain to herb and vegetable gardens.

400 S Walton Blvd., Bentonville, 479-273-3636
peelcompton.org/visit-peel

UNDERSTAND WHAT SHAPED THIS AREA
AT THE ROGERS HISTORICAL MUSEUM

The Rogers Historical Museum, celebrating its 50th anniversary in 2025, is two museums in one. Five permanent galleries talk about the history and geography of Benton County and this region. The exhibits where I was most fascinated and educated were *White River*, which explained the why, when, where, and how of Beaver Lake and Monte Ne, and *Natural State*, detailing Arkansas's geography, geology, and conservation efforts. *Our Place*, *Road and Rail*, and *America's Heartland* exhibits focus on the people and development in the 19th and 20th centuries.

Across the street is the Hawkins House, a historic house museum. Running water was not available when the house was built in 1895, but the downtown middle-class Victorian home did have electricity. It has been restored true to the early 1900s with period wallpaper and decor. Three pieces of furniture are original to the home; other antique furniture was donated by area families.

313 S 2nd St., Rogers, 479-621-1154
rogershistoricalmuseum.org

IMMERSE YOURSELF IN THE MOMENT

AT THE MOMENTARY

I used to think the Momentary was modern art, but this extension of Crystal Bridges Museum of American Art is rather "art of the moment" or present art, including culinary and performance art. I find that the visual arts at the Momentary mean more when I start chatting with a volunteer docent about the art and artist. The story and the thoughts behind the art enrich the experience.

The Momentary also brings award-winning, top-of-their-field performers in many music genres to Bentonville, as well as new faces. The music may come in multiday festivals or a concert and are well worth getting on the Momentary email list to hear when tickets become available.

There are several options for food and drinks, starting with coffee at Onyx Coffee Lab and in the Tower Bar, where views extend into the rolling hills. Later, the Tower Bar switches to handcrafted cocktails and the outdoor RØDE Bar opens on the patio.

507 SE E St., Bentonville, 479-367-7500
themomentary.org

ENVISION A 200-YEAR-OLD MILL

AT WAR EAGLE MILL

War Eagle Mill was first built in 1832 and was rebuilt three times after the Civil War and floods took the building. The present mill is the 1832 design, rebuilt after a 2015 flood. Although the building was a total loss, the system of hoisting the 50-year-old equipment from the beams when a flood is imminent saved the gristmill. It is only used for scheduled demonstrations now, commanding the corner of the main floor, where corn and flour meal, canned goods, and items by local artisans are sold.

Upstairs is a café with a delicious country menu. You may find beans and corn bread, fried chicken, mac and cheese, or biscuits on the menu, which to me sounds like fine dining.

This is a fun place to wander with a camera, inside and out. Check their website for seasonal and weather closures.

11045 War Eagle Rd., Rogers, 479-520-7044
visitwareaglemill.com

TIP

War Eagle Craft Fair started in 1954 to showcase both local crafts and fall foliage. Decades later, it is still a popular event each October and has inspired many other craft fairs in the area.

wareaglefair.com

FOCUS ON ONE PART OF THE SKY

INSIDE JAMES TURRELL'S SKYSPACE, *THE WAY OF COLOR*

A skyspace is a room with part of the ceiling open to the sky. More than 80 skyspaces by artist James Turrell have been installed throughout the world, including the one on the Crystal Bridges Art Trail, which opened in 2009. As the sun is rising and after it sets, LED lights slowly change color inside the chamber. The oculus open to the sky changes color, too. The inside walls are Arkansas native stone and the heated bench is Kansas limestone.

From a little after sunrise to a little before sunset, the colors are not on. At any time, this is a contemplative spot, with clouds passing and birds flying over the oculus. There may already be a group inside; the circular bench can seat about 24 people. In that case, I hope they break into song. The acoustics are reported to be amazing.

TIP

This is on the southern end of the Crystal Bridges Art Trail and an easy walk from Crystal Bridges Museum, Compton Gardens, or downtown Bentonville. Handicap parking is available on Third Street. Restrooms are nearby. I would suggest staying 45 minutes to experience the changing lights before sunrise and after sunset. The sign outside the chamber entrance tells you what to expect.

75

SEE ARKANSAS'S FIRST AGRI-HOOD

AT RED BARN FARM

Have you ever experienced an agri-hood? Red Barn Farm is a neighborhood of rental units with a wooded area, farm, and community green space. The organic farm one mile north of downtown Bentonville contains row crops plus hoop houses to extend the season. Red Barn Farm sells at the Bentonville Farmers Market, to local restaurants, and through an online order/pickup system. They also roast coffee inside the main farm building.

The community building also includes a self-serve farm stand. Edible landscaping and fire pits are more the norm here than community pools and tennis courts. The red barn that dominates the area is a gathering space for events and rentals. I attended a farm-to-table dining experience created by an area chef and served family style with live music. Follow their socials to find out what events they schedule.

I also volunteer at Red Barn Farm, learning about growing vegetables while helping out.

1601 NW A St., Bentonville, 479-250-1011
redbarnbentonville.com

VOLUNTEER
BECAUSE SO MANY NEED YOU

Do you want to meet like-minded friends? Do you want to learn more about a subject that interests you? Volunteer at a location you love. Do you want to get out of a slump? Help someone else. Do you want to attend a concert or a play without fitting a ticket into your tight budget? Do you feel a bit shy going alone? Events often use volunteers.

This area is rich in museums, animal shelters, gardens, hospice and health care, and various nonprofits. Many have a volunteer coordinator who would be happy to tell you about opportunities on a weekly schedule, seasonally, or as needed for events and special projects. The more you are involved in one community of volunteers, the more options open for you.

bentonvillear.com/545/volunteer-program

Marrs Mercantile

SHOPPING AND FASHION

DISCOVER
8TH STREET MARKET

It is a challenge to describe how amazing 8th Street Market is. The shell structure of this market was a poultry processing plant for three decades, beside a cheese factory. The cheese factory was renovated into the Momentary and the popular Razorback Greenway Trail is beside both. The new Walmart headquarters campus is a short walk away.

The locally owned businesses that make up the 8th Street Market are so special that many have their own entries in this book. Brightwater: A Center for the Study of Food, the culinary school operated by NorthWest Arkansas Community College, and Bike Rack Brewing Co. were the first tenants in 2017. Unique shops balance the eclectic dining options. Outdoor dining areas, the food truck park, a climbing rock, and creative murals make 8th Street Market a gathering place for all ages, with a good mix of families, friends, and solo folks.

801 SE 8th St., Bentonville
8stmarket.com

TIP

While discovering one of the 8th Street shops or restaurants on the facing page, take time to wander around all of 8th Street Market. While you are there, you may want to follow the path that connects to the Momentary.

LOCAL BUSINESSES IN 8TH STREET MARKET

Bike Rack Brewing Co.
Taproom and production brewery
479-319-6593, bikerackbrewing.com

Cocoon Yoga Lab
479-856-9238, cocoonyogalab.com

Co-op
Ozark ramen house with authentic Japanese flavors
479-250-0474, coopramen.com

Hillfolk Textile Studio + Shop
Craft and home goods, yarn, contemporary
and traditional fiber arts classes
479-877-5357, hillfolk.com

Markham & Fitz Chocolate Makers
A locally owned, woman-owned small business that distributes
chocolates to six countries and has won many awards and accolades
479-367-2608, markhamandfitz.com

Sweet Freedom Cheese
Selling an amazing selection of cheeses, plus meats,
spreads, fresh bread, wines, and more
479-268-5867, sweetfreedomcheese.com

Two Friends Bookstore + Cafe
An independent bookstore offering sandwiches and wine
479-367-2442, twofriendsbooks.com

Yeyo's
Mexican restaurant with an award-winning chef
479-657-6954, yeyosnwa.com

Food trucks in the south parking lot

DISCOVER AND SHOP
IN HISTORIC DOWNTOWNS

Both Bentonville and Rogers have vibrant downtowns that offer a variety of shops, museums, restaurants, and parks, plus historic neighborhoods nearby. You can easily spend an afternoon discovering these areas. Both downtowns have celebrated their 1800s historic architecture while encouraging creative restoration, new structures, and pedestrian spaces.

The center of downtown Bentonville is a park the size of a city block. Opposite the county courthouse on one side, the newly renovated Walmart Museum will open in 2025. The Razorback Greenway is on the other side of the county courthouse. Hotels (two are under construction as I write this), B and Bs, and parking garages are within a few blocks.

Rogers's main downtown green space is on the east side, with bike paths, art, a splash pad, and more. Eight blocks of 100-year-old brick-paved streets have been preserved in downtown Rogers, as have significant freestanding historic buildings.

TAKE YOUR COOKING AND YOUR KITCHEN UP A LEVEL
AT HONEYCOMB KITCHEN SHOP

Honeycomb Kitchen Shop carries high-quality brands that they truly believe in, such as Mason Cash, Zwilling, Smithey, and Le Creuset. Their two-story downtown shop sells linens, barware, foods, baking and decorating supplies, and more.

Next door is their teaching kitchen, where two dozen students can watch the teacher and screens and work together in small teams for hands-on cooking.

If you are interested in taking their very popular cooking classes, ranging from cocktails to ethnic dishes to baking to knife skills, it's a three-step process:

1. Get on their email list.
2. As soon as you get notifications of upcoming classes, review and choose
3. Register ASAP, because these classes sell out quickly!

213 W Walnut St., Rogers, 479-340-1022
honeycombkitchenshop.com

WALK INTO THE SHOWROOM
OF A.G. RUSSELL KNIVES

You can't miss the large A.G. Russell Knives building on the 1-49 Pleasant Grove exit, south of Rogers. Part of that is the only showroom of this country's first knife mail-order business, started on A.G. Russell's kitchen table in 1964.

When it comes to knives, A.G. Russell is a legend. According to the website, he is responsible for the concept and promotion of the Knifemakers' Guild for handmade knifemakers, the first knife collectors' club, the first limited-edition, serial-numbered knives, and more.

Inside the showroom there are knives designed by A.G. Russell and folding knives, but also fishing fillet knives, kitchen cutlery, and more. There is also a display of their Russell's for Men products (russellsformen.com), including clothing, cologne, and things for the office, travel, workshop, and more.

2900 S 26th St., Rogers, 479-631-0130
agrussell.com

SHOW YOUR LOYALTY
AT BENTONVILLE MERCANTILE AND ROGERS MERCANTILE

Hats, T-shirts, stickers, books, and home decor proudly celebrating Bentonville and Rogers (and area towns, such as Bella Vista) abound in these locally owned stores. There also is a large selection of handmade jewelry, wood crafts, candles, foods, toys, stationery, and more filling the shelves. Of course, Arkansas Razorbacks and regional sports team themes can be found here, too.

Bentonville Mercantile and Rogers Mercantile (and the Fayetteville Mercantile) work with over 100 Northwest Arkansas makers so that their products represent not only local towns but local artists and small businesses. Each store has its own character and is constantly bringing in new makers and products. This store is the epitome of "shop local" and a great place to shop for gifts, online or in the store. (In the store is more fun.)

103 SE 2nd St., Bentonville, 479-326-0682
1501 SE Walton Blvd., Ste. 109, Bentonville
bentonvillemercantile.com

121S 2nd St., Rogers
Facebook and Instagram: @rogersmercantile

SUPPORT
YOUR LOCAL INDEPENDENT BOOKSTORE

If you love independent bookstores, you can find one in both Bentonville and Rogers, offering books plus some stationery and gifts.

Two Friends Bookstore is owned by—yes—two friends who are helpful and knowledgeable, as are their staff. Recommendations are posted with the books, and book lovers gather together for book clubs and events. This bookstore in Bentonville's popular 8th Street Market is also a café with a menu that includes sandwiches, cookies, coffees, beers, and wines. The sandwiches are made fresh with bread from a local bakery.

Brick walls, comfy seating, extended hours, and helpful staff help make Underbrush Books in downtown Rogers feel like a retreat into a friend's private library. Book clubs, events, and beverages are available.

Two Friends Bookstore + Cafe
801 SE 8th St., Ste. 47, Bentonville, 479-367-2442
twofriendsbooks.com

Underbrush Books
103 W Walnut St., Rogers, 479-507-4227
underbrushbooks.com

LUCKILY, BENTONVILLE AND ROGERS ARE RICH IN BOOKSTORES TO DISCOVER.

Once Upon a Time Books
Well-curated used bookstore also has a large inventory that you can order online and pick up in the store
116 W Central Ave., Bentonville, 479-367-2595
onceuponatimebooks.com

The Friendly Bookstore
This Friends of the Rogers Public Library used bookstore is a treasure. See next entry.
1114 W Poplar Pl., Rogers, 479-246-0533
friendlybookstore.org

Read It Again Bookstore
Used books for sale inside the Bentonville Public Library and at an annual book sale fundraiser
405 S Main St., Bentonville

Barnes & Noble
Familiar nationwide bookstore includes a café
261 N 46th St., Rogers, 479-636-2002
stores.barnesandnoble.com/store/2134

WANDER ROOMFULS OF USED BOOKS
AT THE FRIENDLY BOOKSTORE

Wow! The Rogers Public Library has a lot of friends! Friends who donate and organize books and staff this all-volunteer, nonprofit bookstore.

A library bookstore is often in a cart outside the gift shop or in a small room, but this bookstore is a building in itself—many rooms of books. I always start in Room #2 with the cookbooks and garden books, tote bag in hand. Then I head to Room #6 with art and travel books. At these prices, I find a couple books to leaf through on my patio before returning them as a donation. Books must be donated from my home to make room for the ones I keep. It's a lovely cycle.

The readers I am most impressed with are the excited kids who get to choose a few "new" books. Mom and Dad find a few, too.

1114 W Poplar Pl., Rogers, 479-246-0533
friendlybookstore.org

SHOP METAPHYSICAL
AT THE SAGE ELEPHANT

This metaphysical store includes crystals, incense, jewelry, essential oils, tarot cards, a large collection of stones, clothing, home decor, and more. Their staff are more than happy to give insightful answers to your questions. There is a meeting space beside the store for sound baths, a healing circle, meditation, or to bring in a local or regional intuitive, tarot card reader, etc. for appointments. Follow them on social media to hear about their events, including Full Moon Drum Circles.

Whether you are very into this, interested but confused, or want to know a bit more on one subject, this is a calming, welcoming store.

120 N 13th St., Rogers, 479-202-5089
thesageelephant.store

DONATE AND SHOP TO EMPOWER OTHERS

AT BEAUTIFUL LIVES THRIFT BOUTIQUE

Beautiful Lives Thrift Boutique, which was started in Fayetteville by Melody Taylor and New Heights Church Fayetteville, now has four Northwest Arkansas locations. Each store, including the Bentonville location, is an upscale thrift store curated with gently used items with boutique displays and service. Special sales at the beginning of a season grant early access to ticket holders.

Not only does the relaxing boutique environment empower women, but this store donates to nonprofits, helps outfit women needing a fresh start, and provides employment. Donating clothing that you no longer use helps to support Beautiful Lives' mission. In return, you can declutter your closets and find a great new item in the same trip.

The Global Shoppe inside the store sells handcrafted products from around the world. Sales support artisans who create these items.

1327 S Main St., Bentonville, 479-553-7237
beautifullivesboutique.com

RELAX, DINNER INSPIRATION CAN BE FOUND AT BENTONVILLE PROVISIONS

Imagine a spot where you can pick up dinner on the way home. And you can also pick up flowers, local produce, or fresh bread in this spacious, sunny store. If you wish, you can sit down and have a glass of wine and chat. Maybe that chat is about their upcoming cooking demonstrations and classes that you want to attend or that cookware that caught your eye.

You could stop by for a sandwich at lunch and pick up a few supplies that inspire you to create dinner later, one of the many spices and sauces or a cookbook on the shelf. Bentonville Provisions is a pantry, gift store, and a lunch/wine counter that has a neighborhood vibe.

406 SE 5th St., Ste. 4, Bentonville, 479-685-0600
bentonville-provisions.com

BUY
YOUR PUPPY A PRESENT
AT THREE DOG BAKERY

Looking for a special something for someone you love—someone with four paws and a wagging tail? Discover a dog boutique with supplies, food, toys, clothes, and more in both downtown Bentonville and downtown Rogers.

The focal point of Three Dog Bakery in Bentonville is a display case of beautiful, baked-in-shop dog treats. For a major event, they can bake a cake for dog training graduation or adoption day. It is also a toy store for pups. Toys and pupcakes—that gets tails wagging.

113 W Central Ave., Bentonville, 479-268-5599
threedogstores.com/bakery/bentonville-square

TIP

Another great place to bring your dog is Woof and Wander in downtown Rogers. Woof and Wander has a self-serve dog wash station and the store includes natural treats and holistic supplements, plus pet accessories, greeting cards, and more created by local artisans. Make sure you book the station in advance.

BROWSE AMONG BEAUTIFUL THINGS
AT COBBLESTONE & VINE

Cobblestone & Vine opened in Little Rock over 30 years ago. They opened their Bentonville location over three years ago. This is an interior design store and gift shop with a staff who is just as welcoming to someone stopping by between picking up pet food at Tractor Supply and dropping off donations at Helping Hands Thrift Store (me) as they are to someone creating a wedding registry.

This upscale home boutique offers furniture, lamps, chandeliers, vases, dinnerware, linens, candles, and an amazing collection of design books. They also carry jewelry, lotions, and holiday decor. They can help you find a perfect piece of furniture or a special gift or help with your interior design. Everything in Cobblestone & Vine is beautiful and beautifully displayed. Sometimes 15 minutes surrounded by beautiful things is what your day needs.

2812 S Walton Blvd., Bentonville, 479-319-8040
cobblestoneandvine.com

FIND OR MAKE AN EVERLASTING ARRANGEMENT AT COMMON DWELLINGS

This florist specializes in wood flowers, which last forever and don't trigger allergies. I love fresh flowers and always have them in my house, but an everlasting arrangement has its place, too. Imagine a lasting memory from a special celebration. Step inside of Common Dwellings and you can see the possibilities with wood flowers. Shop among the arrangements, planters, wreaths, and even hats in this florist shop.

Even better, register for one of their evening classes to create your own arrangement, hat, wreath, planter, etc. Some classes are BYOB, so sip and create, get to know a few new people, then take home what you've just made. Many projects celebrate holidays and seasons. This would be a different Girls Night Out or mother-daughter experience. They also offer a kids' class one Saturday afternoon a month.

1401 SE Walton Blvd., Ste. 205, Bentonville, 815-351-1470
commondwellings.com

SHOP LOCAL
AT DOWNTOWN FARMERS MARKETS

You can meet a lot of local talent offering their creations at farmers markets, people who grow, bake, craft, and more. Bentonville's market is around the downtown square, extending down side streets. Rogers's market is at Railyard Park east of downtown. During the cold season, both markets move to nearby indoor locations. Follow their social media accounts to hear about special days, live music, and winter locations.

Arrive early to choose from the best selection. Later in the morning there may be music and the downtown stores and restaurants will be open.

Try both markets. Both have fruits and vegetables, meats and cheeses, flowers, baked goods, and arts and crafts, but each is a bit different. Bentonville has more booths and lots of people. Rogers is smaller and easier to chat with vendors, plus I can get my pruners sharpened at a Rogers booth.

Bentonville Farmers Market
downtownbentonville.org/event/fm

Rogers Local Food & Art Market
rogerslocalfoodmarket.com

KEEP YOUR CRAFTING MUSE AMUSED
AT HILLFOLK TEXTILE STUDIO + SHOP

If you love textiles and handcrafted items, let your muse lead you to Hillfolk. Part shop, part studio, and filled with inspiration, this store manages to calm you down and get you excited at the same time. Perhaps it is the yarn display, the handmade items you just must touch, the inspiring books, the fragrance of the handmade candles, or the class happening around the large table in the back of the shop. Classes taught at Hillfolk range from quilting to watercolor to dyeing to spinning. Or you can buy a kit and try a new craft at home.

Hillfolk is more than a store; it is a community. One visit or one class and you are a part of this community.

Hey, you artful soul: The Momentary is a short walk down a gravel path from this shop. Your muse is going to be so happy!

801 SE 8th St., Ste. 49, Bentonville, 479-877-5357
hillfolk.com

FIND A UNIQUE GIFT
AT KALEIDOSCOPE COLLECTIVE

Kaleidoscope Collective is a downtown retail space for local artists creating handmade items.

Art types and styles range as wide as the creative minds in this collective. The store is set up so that an artist's work is grouped together, but as a boutique. One artist's jewelry may be sharing a table with purses or stationery by a printmaker. You may find an original framed painting hanging beside stained-glass mirrors. If you find unique gifts, they will gift wrap your purchases for you.

Visit their Facebook page to get a feel for the workshops held by artisan artists, and then sign up to try jewelry making, rug tufting, or another fun craft.

They are always open for Downtown Rogers Art on the Bricks the second Thursday of each month, so make sure to stop in.

109 W Walnut St., Rogers
kaleidoscopecollective.store

93

BREATHE IN
AT THE LITTLE CANDLE OF NWA

The Little Candle of NWA sells many of their hand-poured, soy wax candles to stores and online, but you can walk in and try all their scents at their storefront in downtown Rogers. There are several scents to choose from, such as Mahogany Teakwood and Grapefruit Rind.

However, their signature candles are scents created and named for this area—scents like Northwest Arkansas, Bella Vista, Beaver Lake, and Ozark Trails.

The Bentonville candle is a blend of clementine and jasmine.

The Rogers candle is a blend of grapefruit, cardamon, and cedar.

This would be a perfect gift for a new neighbor or to send a recent college graduate to remind them of home. Or enjoy one in your home. Each of the signature candles lasts for about 70 hours.

112 N 3rd St., Rogers, 949-702-1620
shoplittlecandleco.com

SHOP INSIDE A *FIXER TO FABULOUS* RENOVATION AT MARRS MERCANTILE

You never know what treasures you will find in Marrs Mercantile. Fans of the HGTV shows hosted by Jenny and Dave Marrs must visit this store curated with the *Fixer to Fabulous* (*F2F*) flair. Of course, they keep signed copies of Jenny's book in stock. They also have many items to inspire self-care, dinner parties, and thoughtful gifts. Local artisan goods and foods, books about this area, and items for children can also be found here. Recent episodes showing a renovation in Italy provide the benefit of Italian olive oil and handcrafted Italian goods being featured in the store.

The store is in the renovated 1905 Centerton Bank, with a glass front wall and high ceiling, creating a spacious, bright boutique setting. The patio to the side has seating and a play structure.

289 N Main St., Centerton
marrsmercantile.com

MORE FOR *FIXER TO FABULOUS* FANS

The visitor center in Bentonville has a life-size cutout for selfies and recently printed a brochure mapping *Fixer to Fabulous* homes and listing Jenny's favorite shops and antique stores. Many renovated homes are in Rogers, too. If you go on the Big on Bentonville Golf Cart Tour, your guide will be happy to point out *F2F* homes.

The Welcome Inn
You can take a virtual tour online and rent the three-bedroom Airbnb renovated on *Fixer to Fabulous*.
1206 S 11th St., Rogers
thewelcomeinn.co

Annual Berry Fest at The Berry Farm
Every June, people bring their buckets to this U-pick organic blueberry farm and enjoy live music, artists, vendors, and food trucks at this fundraiser.
12627 Huber Rd., Bentonville
theberryfarmbentonville.com

Jenny and Dave Marrs are very involved in area communities and feature local businesses on their show. You may have seen Dave and Jenny visit **Challalujah Bakery** on a few *F2F* episodes. Here you'll find organic baked goods with gluten-free, sugar-free, and keto options. Their cinnamon rolls and dairy-free breads are very popular for a reason.
271 N Main St., Centerton
challalujahbakery.com

95

FIND THE PERFECT PRESENT
AT AREA MUSEUM GIFT SHOPS

Museums place their gift shops near the entrance, which in our area is also near free parking. There is no reason not to think of museum gift shops when you are shopping for the perfect gift. You can browse among local crafts, history and art books, jewelry, and educational toys.

My favorites? Peel Museum and War Eagle Mill for local crafts and foods. For books about regional history, turn to Rogers Historical Museum, Bella Vista Museum, Pea Ridge National Military Park, and the Museum of Native American History. They all have a large selection of history and regional books.

For educational toys, Hobbs State Park, Amazeum, and Crystal Bridges are excellent. Also strong on educational toys are the Thaden Fieldhouse gift shop and War Eagle Cavern gift shop.

Almost every museum gift shop includes jewelry, but especially Crystal Bridges, the Momentary, and the Museum of Native American History.

Scott Family Amazeum
1009 Museum Way (J Street and Museum Way), Bentonville

Bella Vista Historical Museum
1885 Bella Vista Way, Bella Vista

Crystal Bridges Museum of American Art
600 Museum Way, Bentonville

Hobbs State Park-Conservation Area
20201 E Hwy. 12, Rogers

The Momentary
507 SE E St., Bentonville

Museum of Native American History
202 SW O St., Bentonville

Pea Ridge National Military Park
15930 National Park Dr., Garfield

Peel Museum & Botanical Garden
400 S Walton Blvd., Bentonville

Rogers Historical Museum
313 S 2nd St., Rogers

Thaden Fieldhouse
2205 SW I St., Bentonville

War Eagle Cavern
21494 Cavern Dr., Rogers

War Eagle Mill
11045 War Eagle Rd., Rogers

SHOP FAIR-TRADE
AT REMEDY ROAD

Remedy Road is a downtown boutique that supports makers and artisans worldwide by carrying and supporting fair-trade and ethical brands. Many of the goods you find in this shop are handcrafted items or unique designs.

Proceeds from this shop are then donated to nonprofits that support artisans and ensure fair wages, plus a percentage is donated to nonprofits in this area. The store carries an eclectic selection of purses, totes, clothing, jewelry, candles, stationery, gifts, and more, beautifully displayed.

The back room is a different selection though. Remedy Closet is filled with donated clothes that are for sale and available for women who need clothes to wear to work or interviews. Customers can donate clothes for Remedy Closet to earn discounts in Remedy Road.

112 W Central Ave., Bentonville, 479-321-1316
shopremedyroad.com

FILL YOUR PANTRY WITH FLAVOR
AT THE HOUSE OF WEBSTER GIFT SHOP

The House of Webster creates jellies, salsas, syrups, dressings, and more in their facilities north of downtown Rogers. This company, which has been a part of Rogers since 1934, ships nationwide under its own labels and creates custom brand labels for familiar stores and destination gift shops.

While you are looking at labels, read the ingredients list. The words are easy to pronounce, and many products have four to six ingredients packaged into old-fashioned canning jars. Yes, you can get strawberry jelly and orange marmalade but also muscadine jelly, pickled beets, Ozark stout ale mustard, and butter-pecan syrup. Some salsas and spreads can turn up the heat.

Most people order from their website, but the local gift shop cabin offers a large selection of their products, plus cheeses, bacon, kitchen towels, and more. Let them help you create and ship a gift box or fill a gift basket for a friend while you are there to stock your own pantry.

1013 N 2nd St., Rogers, 800-369-4641
houseofwebster.com

CREATE A CHARCUTERIE BOARD

AT SWEET FREEDOM CHEESE

Sweet Freedom Cheese is Arkansas's first independent cut-to-order cheese shop. Their cheesemongers all want to help you love and understand cheese and almost all have culinary degrees. They are happy to explain the differences, recommend cheeses to suit your taste, and offer samples to taste. That desire to serve both the public and producers of artisanal food is part of why Sweet Freedom Cheese was listed in *Wine Enthusiast* magazine's "10 Most Iconic Cheese Shops in America" in 2023.

Their shop also includes wine, small-batch brews, cured meats, locally made bread, and a selection of gourmet and local pantry supplies—everything you need to create a gift basket, plan a party, stock your pantry, or enjoy a relaxing evening.

Sweet Freedom Cheese can create an indulgent lunch for you. Their menu contains an assortment of cheese plates or made-to-order grilled cheese sandwiches. Beverages on the menu include wines and beers.

801 SE 8th St., Ste. 1, Bentonville, 479-268-5867
sweetfreedomcheese.com

Museum Store at Peel Museum & Botanical Garden

BROWSE LOCAL AND REGIONAL ARTS AND CRAFTS

AT WISHING SPRING GALLERY & GIFT SHOP

This three-story gallery in a restored barn (check out the historical photos on the wall) has been operating since 1984. The Artisan Alliance, an active nonprofit formed in 1966, runs this shop that showcases art and crafts by more than 40 artisans in the alliance.

This is an eclectic gallery that is fun to browse. Artwork ranges from stunning paintings to creative ceramics to holiday ornaments to fine jewelry to quilts. You can travel from historic crafts to modern art in this large gallery.

Adding to the sense of community is the Clay Studio, in the building behind the gallery. Here, ceramics artists ranging from beginner on help each other learn and grow. Equipment in this workshop includes eight wheels and three kilns. Classes, workshops, and more information can be found at the-clay-studio.square.site.

8862 W McNelly Rd., Bentonville, 479-273-1798
wishingspringgallery.net

OTHER GALLERIES SHOWCASING LOCAL ARTISTS

Art on the Square

Art on the Square is an art gallery representing 15 or more very talented artists and craftsmen. Often one of those artists is behind the counter and easy to talk to. Browse original paintings, prints, woodcrafts, jewelry, and more.

102 E Central Ave., Bentonville, 479-685-5271

artonthesquarebentonville.com

Art Collective Gallery

This gallery focuses on contemporary art by local, national, and international artists. They also offer talks open to the public.

228 S 1st St., Rogers, 479-877-5868

artcollectivegallery.com

100

SAVE MONEY, LIVE BETTER
AT WALMART SUPERCENTER STORE #0001

You're in Northwest Arkansas, where Walmart started. Why not visit Walmart Supercenter Store #0001 in Rogers? However, it's not the first Walmart store location. That opened in 1962 in Rogers near 8th and Walnut. Many of my allowances were spent at Wal-Mart Discount City in the 1960s and '70s. Yes, Sam Walton had stores before that, but they were not named Walmart. You can discover the history at the Walmart Museum on the Bentonville Square.

Other area stores include Walmart Supercenter #100 (406 S Walton Blvd., Bentonville), close to the headquarters, or Walmart Supercenter #5260 (4208 Pleasant Crossing Blvd., Rogers), an upscale area location with an in-store sushi restaurant.

Some area Walmart stores offer drone delivery and/or in-store community health clinics.

Although Sam's Club is a division of Walmart and headquartered in Bentonville, too, the first location was in Oklahoma. The first Neighborhood Market was in Bentonville.

2110 W Walnut St., Rogers, 479-636-3222
walmart.com/store/1-rogers-ar

ACTIVITIES
BY SEASON

SPRING

Get Gardening Advice at the Benton County Master Gardener Association Plant Sale, 52

Appreciate Nature at Compton Gardens and Arboretum, 82

Get Outdoors with 37 North Expeditions, 46

Watch the Planes While Having Lunch at Louise, 10

Listen to Classical Piano at the Van Cliburn Concerts, 39

SUMMER

Celebrate Summer Downtown at the Railyard Live Concert Series, 36

Join the Party at First Fridays in Downtown Bentonville, 28

Be a Part of the Annual Bentonville Film Festival, 31

Be Cool Underground at War Eagle Cavern, 47

FALL

Walk around the Lake at Lake Atalanta Park, 55

Enjoy the Ride at Bikes, Blues & BBQ Motorcycle Rally, 51

Stroll Downtown Rogers during Art on the Bricks, 30

Tour a Frank Lloyd Wright Design at the Bachman-Wilson House, 75

WINTER

Skate or Splash at Lawrence Plaza, 69

Watch a Parade, 35

Take a Selfie with the *World's Largest BB Gun* at the Daisy Airgun Museum, 84

Buy Your Puppy a Present at Three Dog Bakery, 110

Support Your Local Independent Bookstore, 104

SUGGESTED ITINERARIES

EXPLORE HWY 12 TO BEAVER LAKE

Indulge in Award-Winning Fried Chicken at Monte Ne Inn, 12

Envision a 200-Year-Old Mill at War Eagle Mill, 91

Feel at Home in Jaclyn's Kitchen, 9

Get on a Trail at Hobbs State Park-Conservation Area, 66

Be Cool Underground at War Eagle Cavern, 47

DATE NIGHT

Stroll Downtown Rogers during Art on the Bricks, 30

Get Comfy at Skylight Cinema, 37

Listen to Classical Piano at the Van Cliburn Concerts, 39

Take Aim at the Quiver Archery, 68

Fly Above Bentonville and Rogers from Thaden Field, 61

Buy Original Art from an Art-o-mat® Vending Machine, 74

Discover 8th Street Market, 98

Discover and Shop in Historic Downtowns, 100

Move to the Music at Walmart AMP (Arkansas Music Pavilion), 42

FOR THE WHOLE FAMILY

Watch the Planes While Having Lunch at Louise, 10

Grab an Extra Napkin at Wright's Barbecue, 23

Get Outdoors with 37 North Expeditions, 46

Plan a Pizza Night Out at Gusano's Chicago-Style Pizzeria, 7

Join the Party at First Fridays in Downtown Bentonville, 28

Be Cool Underground at War Eagle Cavern, 47

Buy Original Art from an Art-o-mat® Vending Machine, 74

Walk around the Lake at Lake Atalanta Park, 55

Skate or Splash at Lawrence Plaza, 69

Get Hands-On at the Scott Family Amazeum, 73

Get on a Trail at Hobbs State Park-Conservation Area, 66

BUY LOCAL ART

Breathe In at the Little Candle of NWA, 117

Shop Local at Downtown Farmers Markets, 114

Find a Unique Gift at Kaleidoscope Collective, 116

Browse Local and Regional Arts and Crafts at Wishing Spring Gallery & Gift Shop, 126

Keep Your Crafting Muse Amused at Hillfolk Textile Studio + Shop, 115

HGTV'S *FIXER TO FABULOUS* FANS

Shop inside a *Fixer to Fabulous* Renovation at Marrs Mercantile, 118

Discover Bentonville with a Guide with Big on Bentonville Tours, 85

Walk Inside Your Local Visitor Center, 41

IMPRESSIVE ARCHITECTURE

Tour a Frank Lloyd Wright Design at the Bachman-Wilson House, 75

Listen to Classical Piano at the Van Cliburn Concerts, 39

Focus on One Part of the Sky inside James Turrell's Skyspace, *The Way of Color*, 92

Experience the Architecture of E. Fay Jones in Bella Vista, 76

See Two Different Homes from the 1800s at the Peel Museum & Botanical Garden, 88

Bike, Walk, or Camp in Coler Mountain Bike Preserve, 54

Envision a 200-Year-Old Mill at War Eagle Mill, 91

Get on a Trail at Hobbs State Park-Conservation Area, 66

TIME WITH A FRIEND

Walk with a New Best Friend at Best Friends Pet Resource Center, 50

Take Your Cooking and Your Kitchen up a Level at Honeycomb Kitchen Shop, 101

Take Aim at the Quiver Archery, 68

Travel from Bella Vista to Fayetteville on the Razorback Regional Greenway Trail, 62

Discover Bentonville with a Guide with Big on Bentonville Tours, 85

Shop Local at Downtown Farmers Markets, 114

Focus on One Part of the Sky inside James Turrell's Skyspace, *The Way of Color*, 92

Slow Down along the Art Trail at Crystal Bridges, 48

Find or Make an Everlasting Arrangement at Common Dwellings, 113

Relax with a Cigar at Black Crown Social Cigar & Whiskey Lounge, 32

HISTORY BUFFS

Learn about a Decisive Civil War Battle at Pea Ridge National Military Park, 87

Learn about the Early Years at the Bentonville History Museum, 79

Understand What Shaped This Area at the Rogers Historical Museum, 89

Be Cool Underground at War Eagle Cavern, 47

Travel through Time at the Museum of Native American History, 86

Discover a Varied History at Bella Vista Historical Museum, 78

See Two Different Homes from the 1800s at the Peel Museum & Botanical Garden, 88

NATURE

Get Outdoors with 37 North Expeditions, 46

Bike, Walk, or Camp in Coler Mountain Bike Preserve, 54

Slow Down along the Art Trail at Crystal Bridges, 48

Be Cool Underground at War Eagle Cavern, 47

Fly Above Bentonville and Rogers from Thaden Field, 61

Get Gardening Advice at the Benton County Master Gardener Association Plant Sale, 52

Appreciate Nature at Compton Gardens and Arboretum, 82

Get on a Trail at Hobbs State Park-Conservation Area, 66

Downtown Rogers

INDEX

1907, The, 25
211 Cafe, 79
21c Museum Hotel, 69, 72
37 North Expeditions, 46
7 Brew, 2
A New American Town podcast, 38
A.G. Russell Knives, 102
Airship coffee shop, 54, 58
Alkhatib, Chef Khaled, 20
Alkhatib, Chef Sal, 20
America's Best Restaurants, 9
Annual Berry Fest at the Berry Farm, 119
Applegate Trail, 54
Arkansas Public Theatre, 40
Arkansas Quartz Crystals, 81
Art Collective Gallery, 127
Art on the Bricks, 30, 116
Art on the Square, 127
Art-o-mat® vending machines, 74
Artisan Wood Fired Kitchen, 3
Bachman-Wilson House, 75, 81
Baked by Kori, 4

Barnes & Noble, 105
Beautiful Lives Thrift Boutique, 108
Beaver Lake, 9, 12–13, 47, 61, 89, 117
Bella Vista, 7, 38, 62, 65, 76, 78, 82, 103, 117, 120–121
Bella Vista Community Television, 38
Bella Vista Country Club, 76
Bella Vista Historical Museum, 78, 121
Benton County Master Gardener Association, 52
Bentonville Film Festival, 31, 34, 37, 38
Bentonville History Museum, 79
Bentonville History Walking Tour, 79
Bentonville Mercantile, 103
Bentonville Parks and Recreation, 60, 69
Bentonville Provisions, 109
Bentonville Public Library, 105
Bentonville Taco & Tamale Co., 17
Bentonville Visitor's Center, 18
Best Friends Pet Resource Center, Northwest Arkansas, 50
Big on Bentonville tours, 85, 119
Bike Rack Brewing Co., 98–99
Bikes, Blues & BBQ Motorcycle Rally, 51
Black Crown Social Cigar & Whiskey Lounge, 32
Brightwater: A Center for the Study of Food, 98
Buffalo River, 82
BV Bar & Grill, 76

Camping, 46, 54, 66
Centerton, 118–119
Challalujah Bakery, 119
Cigar District, The, 33
Civil War, 87, 88, 91
Clay Studio, The, 126
Co-op, 99
Cobblestone & Vine, 112
Cocoon Yoga Lab, 99
Coler Mountain Bike Preserve, 54
Common Dwellings, 113
Compton, Dr. Neil, 82
Compton Gardens and Arboretum, 82
Concerts, 4, 36, 39, 40, 42, 90, 95
Conifer, xvi, 5
Cooper, Chef Matthew, 5
Crystal Bridges Art Trail, xiv, 23, 92–93
Crystal Bridges Museum of American Art, 6, 39, 48–49, 60, 75, 77, 81, 90, 121
Daisy Airgun Museum, 84
Davis, Geena, 31
Dombek, George, 22
Drone delivery, 43, 128
DWTN Now, 38
Eleven, 6

Entertainment District, 30, 36
Farmers markets, 79, 94, 114
Fassi's Friends Junior Clinic, 57
First Fridays, 28
Fixer to Fabulous, 85, 118–119
Fountains at Lawrence Plaza, The, 69
Friendly Bookstore, The, 105, 106
Glow Run, 60
Gusano's Chicago-Style Pizzeria, 7
Hillfolk Textile Studio + Shop, 99, 115
Hive, The, 72
Hobbs State Park-Conservation Area, 66, 121
Honeycomb Kitchen Shop, 101
House of Webster, The, 123
Iron Horse Coffee Company, 8
Jaclyn's Kitchen, 9
James Beard Award Semifinalist, 5, 24
Jones, E. Fay, 76–77
Kaleidoscope Collective, 116
Lake Atalanta Park, 55, 56
Lake Bentonville, 10, 67
Lawrence Plaza, 69
Ledger, 37, 58–59
Little Candle of NWA, The, 117
Louise, 10

Making Change, 72
Maman, xiv, 48
Markham & Fitz Chocolate Makers, 99
Marrs, Jenny and Dave, 118–119
Marrs Mercantile, 96, 118
Meteor, The, 18
Meteor Guitar Gallery, 34
Mildred B. Cooper Memorial Chapel, 76
Momentary, The, 18, 60, 74, 90, 98, 115, 120–121
Monte Ne, 13, 89
Monte Ne Inn, 12
Museum of Native American History, 86, 120–121
Nola's Pantry, vi, 14
NorthWest Arkansas Community College, 64, 98
Olly Makes Bakery, 16
Once Upon a Time Books, 105
One Eyed Jacks, 33
Onyx Coffee Lab, 6, 90
Osage Park, 10–11, 67, 68, 80
Ozark Beer Company, 15
Ozark Plateau Trail, 66
Parades, 35
Pea Ridge, 35, 87
Pea Ridge National Military Park, 87, 120–121
Peel, Colonel Samuel West, 88

Peel Museum & Botanical Garden, 88, 120–121, 125
Pinnacle Hills, 3, 42
Pinnacle Hills Promenade, 29
Preacher's Son, The, 22
Rail, The, 19
Railyard, The, 56
Railyard Bike Park, 32
Railyard Live concert series, 36
Railyard Loop, 14
Razorback Greenway, 18, 23, 44, 48, 62, 82, 98, 100
Read It Again Bookstore, 105
Red Barn Farm, 94
Red Ryder, 84
Remedy Road, 122
Rink at Lawrence Plaza, The, 69
Rios, Chef Rafael, 24
RØDE Bar, 90
Rogers Historical Museum, 13, 70, 89, 120–121
Rogers Little Theater, 40
Rogers Mercantile, 103
Rogers Public Library, 15, 105, 106
Rogers Short Film Festival, 40
Run Bentonville Half Marathon, 60
Run Bentonville Race Series, 60
Russell's for Men, 102

Sage Elephant, The, 107
Sagmeister, Stefan, 59
Scott Family Amazeum, 73, 120–121
Skylight Cinema, 37
Skyspace, 48, 92
Square 2 Square Bike Ride, 63
Sweet Freedom Cheese, 99, 124
Thaden, Louise, 10, 61, 78
Thaden Field at the Bentonville Municipal Airport, 61, 67
Thaden Fieldhouse, 10–11, 61, 67, 120–121
Third Space Coffee, 50
Thorncrown Chapel, 76
Three Dog Bakery, 110
Toot Beirut Shawarma & More, 20
Tower Bar, The, 90
Turrell, James, 92
Tusk & Trotter American Brasserie, 21
Two Friends Bookstore + Cafe, 99, 104
Underbrush Books, 104
Undercroft, 22
Van Cliburn Concerts, 39
Victory Theater, 4, 26, 40
Virtual reality, 29
Visitor center, 18, 41, 66, 87, 119
Vivace Mediterranean Cuisine, 20

Walmart, 31, 43, 72, 98, 128
Walmart AMP, 42
Walmart Museum, 100, 128
Walmart NWA Championship LPGA Tournament, 57
Walton, Sam and Helen, 79, 128
Walton Arts Center, 42
War Eagle Cavern, 47, 120–121
War Eagle Craft Fair, 91
War Eagle Mill, 91, 120–121
Way of Color, The, 48, 92
Welcome Inn, The, 119
White River, 89
Wishing Spring Gallery & Gift Shop, 126
Woof and Wander, 111
World's Largest BB Gun, 84
Wright, Frank Lloyd, 75, 76–77, 81
Wright's Barbecue, 23
Yeyo's, 24–25, 99